CARRY YOURSELF CAUTIOUSLY ON THE ROADS - YOU ARE TOO PRECIOUS

BE YOUR SAFEST DRIVER

A D JOSHI

First of all, I humbly dedicate this creation to God, for guiding me and showing path to choose a subject, which is a menace to the country – that takes away more than 460 precious lives every day. With God's blessing definitely this book will bring a change in the understanding of common people towards road accidents, which will save many lives on roads.

This book is dedicated to my wife Smitha, who has been a constant inspiration to me for her committment, for standing with me always. Her prayers are always with me and with that courage only I am able to bring the book up to this stage.

This book is dedicated to my both daughters for keeping me motivated and focussed to complete this book.

The book is dedicated to all the families; who lost their beloveds in some road related accidents and who believe that the accident could have been avoided, had there been - a structured driver training infrastructure in our country.

The Book is dedicated to one and all who want to see Indian roads become safe and the number of deaths on the roads should come down from the present rate of more than 430 deaths a day to half of this figure or less in 3 years of time by 2025 ; as envisioned by the Union Ministry of Road Transport and Highways of India.

Contents

Contents

Scanner

Scan for Registration of Online Road Safety session of 2 hours in Hindi and English, based on this Book.

Register for the Course here

You Can Make The Difference

Road Accidents are actually the situations, which a defensive driver can anticipate and prevent, on the road.

Due to lack of proper training, we fail to identify them on the Road.

Preface

On our roads; majority of the drivers are safe drivers, yet they fail to understand the surprises thrown by others and circumstances on the roads – and pay the price. Merely being a safe driver is not sufficient on the roads – One has to be a **Defensive Driver.**

A need for publishing such a book was felt after seeing many actual accidents around us and after going through & analysing the videos that are available in social media. No one really thinks that such a thing can happen to them; it will always happen to others only, is the common feeling among general people.

More than 10000 children under the age of 18 are dying in India - due to road accidents, which mean more than 30 deaths a day. Parents are also responsible for the safety of their wards and they should never allow their minor children to drive on roads and create an unsafe situation for others and for themselves. Many times, parents may not be aware about the outside activities of their children. They should educate their wards about the road safety – without waiting for all them to attain 18 years, as soon as they start moving on roads - alone, for schooling. This way they can prepare them for their responsible behavior on roads when they may away from the eyes of parents with friends.

They should train their children properly through a driving school after they attain the age of 18 and matured enough to understand the hazards on roads. If we give them a vehicle at a younger age, it becomes very difficult for their adolescent mind, to differentiate between a video game and a powerful real machine; they finally would like to win the game only – somehow.

Ignorance about road safety is so deep rooted that very casually people throw away their precious life on roads. Behaviour of drivers on the roads is so careless that the outcome can be just a near miss or an accident only. But we cannot ignore them altogether and leave them to their fate; as, such drivers can create unsafe situations for safe drivers also.

This book has brought out all such situations that are prevalent on our roads.

Today India ranks in number one position; for most number of road accident deaths across 199 countries and accounts for 11% of global deaths due to road accidents. Every year on an average 4, 50,000 road accidents happen in our country, resulting in 1, 50,000 deaths and around 4, 50,000 injuries; many of the injured are permanently disabled.

India is a signatory to the second global high level Conference on Road Safety held in Brazil in 2015, referred to popularly as the **Brasilia Declaration**, which resolved to halve the deaths and injuries from accidents as on 2015, by 2025 and work towards sustainable development by the participating countries by 2030.

The Motor Vehicles Amendment Bill, 2019 was passed by both the Houses of Parliament in August 2019 and has now become an Act. This will improve road safety, enable citizens in their dealings with transport departments smoothly, strengthen rural transport network improvements, public transport and connectivity through automation, computerization and creating awareness.

Online services and efficient, safe and corruption free transport systems in the country will improve the road transport scenario in a big way. India has the second-largest road network in the world, a total of 5.89 million kilometres. This road network transport 64.5% of all goods in the country and 90% of India's total passenger traffic uses the road network only, to commute.

Road transportation has gradually enhanced over the years with better connectivity between cities, towns and villages in the country. Highway construction in India has increased, despite pandemic and lockdown, India has constructed 13,298 km of highways in FY-21. Under the Union Budget 2022-23, the Government of India has allocated Rs. 1,99,107 crore to the Ministry of Road Transport and Highways.

In June 2021, the Ministry of Road Transport and Highways constructed 2,284 KMs of national highways compared with 1,681 KMs in June 2020. The Government of India has allocated Rs. 111 lakh crore under the National Infrastructure Pipeline for FY 2019-25. The road sector is likely to account for 18% capital expenditure over FY 2019-25.

These developments are going to change the road transport scenario in a big way; at the same time with better infrastructure, there will be an increase in the average speed on the roads and if the behavioural aspect of the drivers are not changed, then our country may witness a surge in accidents too.

We have to prepare ourselves for these possibilities and it can be prevented only by spreading awareness. We have to make a system of classroom like teaching, preferably in existing infrastructures; by specially trained professionals for the purpose.

Online format probably may serve the purpose to a large extent - as it is now the most accepted format post COVID scenario.

Foreword

Today *India is in number one position across 199 countries for most road accident related deaths in any country. With only 1% of the total world's vehicles, still contributing for around 11% of Road Accidents worldwide - speaks about the grave scenario we are encountering on our roads daily.* Fatalities on roads not only destroy the family; it has its own impact on the economy of the country also - the nation loses a healthy young workforce too.

A death caused by a disease and if it happens, due to an accident; has entirely different impact on any family. In first case the family will be prepared and it most of the cases, it gives required time to the family to come in terms with the situation. They know the possible outcome and keep themselves mentally ready.

Where as in case of an accident a healthy individual is suddenly taken away from the waiting family; leaving no time to even think - to both, the family and victim. This completely shatters a family.

Roads and associated safety infrastructures are rapidly expanding in our country. So we all collectively have to spread awareness and train our drivers to enhance the overall safety atmosphere on our roads, else the number of accidents may increase due to increase in average speed.

Topping all countries for most crash deaths and injuries is a blackspot on our forehead - we all have to collectively wipe it out.

Henceforth safety on roads will have a new definition in our country; a beginning is made.

Prologue

We need to train them young.

Our present driving licence issuing procedures, mostly focuses on driving skills and to some extent knowledge of road traffic signals. Some trials on roads are conducted in standard format and licences are issued. One to one training happens in the driving schools, where an instructor takes them for trials on roads after imparting basic training in safe locations. These driving training vehicles have double controls and the instructor intervenes when they see an unsafe situation. Instructor both males and females tries their best and most of the drivers learns in the process and do fairly well on actual road conditions too.

The problem comes on roads, when; the lone driver has to react and tackle the real time situations that they encounter. Though there are some standard safe driving practices; which mostly enables the drivers to handle majority of the situations on roads safely; our existing practice is not imparting them to the drivers, elaborately. Finally on the roads, when the driver finds themselves in a situation which demands a prompt manoeuvre to prevent a clash or collision; on occasions; he or she fails to do the right thing.

Driving skill actually warrants drivers to drive in such a way so that unsafe situations are not created - this is the way a defensive driver behaves on the road. But many drivers violate all the norms and when they find themselves in a corner – simply react spontaneously without any clue.

Many of our drivers use only steering or handle to clear the obstacles without ever caring to reduce the speed of the vehicles and this is the major reason for most of our road accidents. Drivers need to monitor their mirrors and surroundings for taking any action, many drivers do it – yet in many of the vehicles they don't maintain the mirrors and indication lamps; particularly the tail lamp.

Some facility should be there in the country that will teach a driver about all these aspects of road safety, our existing setup is definitely not touching these things. In olden times; when vehicles on the roads were less and they were not as powerful as they are now; parents used to teach many tips to their youngsters, now the things have changed; many parents one fine day see their children driving or riding a vehicle somewhere.

Many initiatives are now being taken by governments and road safety is getting the required attention; things will certainly improve. We have been working in this direction for the last 15 years; our educational videos are also available in YouTube.

You will see a huge subscriber's base for accident related videos that happen across the world; but prevention and awareness is actually the need of the hour, to save lives.

Our aim through this book is to make our youngsters a crusader and bring down India's rank from No 1 position in most number of road accidents across the globe. Our present rate of accidents is more than 430 deaths per day, 1 death every 4 minutes; it has to become half - in the next 3 years and even less.

Defensive Driving Pledge

Defensive Driving is a philosophy which if followed religiously will not only save your own life and life of your beloved ones; but it will also improve the overall Road Safety environment on the road in which you are driving.

Before moving ahead please go through the pledges that we are taking to ourselves to improve overall Road Safety of the Country. **I promise that**

1. I am the most important person in the universe and all my actions on the road will be taken to safeguard me. Due to my actions, the safety of others will never be endangered on roads.
2. I will always have consideration for others on the road and I will always respect the right of way of others on the road. My actions on the roads will enhance road safety for me and others.
3. Whenever I see a juction ahead, I will slow down gradually and after ensuring all round safety, then only I must cross the junction.
4. I will follow all the traffic signals and even in any junction if the signals are not there, I will take all my precautions of slowing down, Looking Left and Right and then only I will proceed.
5. I will not start immediately after the signals are becoming GREEN and I will not cross the junction after the signal has gone RED.
6. I will never forget that the Amber or Yellow is a Warning Sign and if the signal is Yellow - I will slow down and will stop before the line, depending upon remaining time in the signal.

7. I will always abide by the rules, whether a traffic authority is there to monitor or not.
8. I will plan my next turn in advance and place myself correctly in a junction for smooth turning
9. I will never overtake inside a junction and I will wait till I cross the junction before overtaking.
10. I will never overspeed and will plan & keep my speed according to road conditions.
11. I understand the importance of regulation of speed in such a way that a need for sudden braking never arises and I plan my speed accordingly.
12. I promise I will never change the lane suddenly.
13. I promise that I will never Overtake in a curved over without planning, I will always wait till I reach a straight stretch.
14. I promise that I will take adequate care before overtaking a Heavy Vehicle.
15. I understand it is my responsibility to keep myself safely away from a Heavy Vehicle.
16. I understand the hazards involved with the open gap between the wheels of a Heavy Vehicle and I will keep myself away from them.
17. I will never move between two running vehicles, till I find a safe passage.
18. I understand the hazards involved in carrying a pillion rider sitting with legs one side and I will take extra precautions.
19. I will stick to the left side of the road, while turning right in a 2 - way road.
20. I will take sufficient rest and will take extra precautions if I have to perform a Night Driving.
21. I very well understand the danger of a closed vehicle.
22. I know how to avoid Highway Hypnosis syndrome.

23. I promise I will never consume alcohol while Driving or drive under the influence of alcohol.
24. While driving or riding I will fully focus on Road and will not allow any distraction.
25. I will not take any abrupt decisions on roads.
26. I will always slow down and if required stop before entering the main road.
27. I will never suddenly slow down or stop in the middle of a highway.
28. I will never drive on the wrong side of the road.
29. I will always ensure that a safe corridor is there in front of me, if not; I will simply slow down.
30. As soon as I see a bridge or a narrow road; immediately I will slow down, and drive safely.
31. I will not blare the horn unnecessarily and will try to drive more with visuals what I see on the road.
32. I will Never block a Free Left turn on the road.
33. I will always keep left in a junction if I have to go straight
34. I will never overtake just before Junction, if I have to turn left after that.
35. I will always use dipper in traffic
36. I will always park the vehicle safely, not obstructing others.
37. Before starting a vehicle from a stationary position I will ensure all safety.
38. I understand that it is always safe to go from behind the animals and I allow them to go freely.
39. I will never carry any loose items in the vehicle, I will secure them properly.
40. I understand the danger of long items being carried in vehicles and keep myself safely away from them.
41. I will wait patiently for my turn on the road and will not disturb the vehicles coming in straight line by

trespassing in their path.

42. I will always take care of the pedestrian on the roads for their safety.

43. I will always slow down in Curves on the roads.

44. I will always be careful of roadside parked vehicles and move carefully while passing along them.

45. I will always slow down while passing through Villages or Thickly populated areas.

46. I will always honor the right of way to the right person who is coming straight and after allowing them only I will move ahead.

47. In a Railway Crossing I will always take all the precautions and will never take any risk.

48. I understand the danger of visibility blockages due to windscreen columns and I take adequate care to ensure that I am able to see my surroundings properly.

49. I will ensure that my vehicle is visible under all climatic conditions, I also ensure that I am able to see all the pedestrians and animals on the road. If visibility is not sufficient I will slow down.

50. I will never take a risk in an overflowing bridge during and for my safety I will wait or detour and take a safer path.

51. I will take all precautions to remain vigilant about the animal movements on the roads.

52. In a Ghat road I will take all the precautions and follow all safety rules.

53. I promise that I will use all the protective gears while riding or driving the vehicle like helmet and Seat Belt.

CHAPTER ONE

DESIGN FLAWS

Whatever may be the design faults on the roads; if a driver takes precautions he can prevent many accidents; all he has to do is think and take actions in advance; he should use his vision for the purpose.

Always drivers may not be at fault; sometimes our road conditions and its design also may cause an accident. **However, whatever may be the condition of the road; the driver ultimately is the final person; who can prevent an accident.**

Since all the controls are with him, he has to observe his surroundings; which includes – all other vehicles on the roads, other occupants, road conditions, climate, visibility and then only take appropriate actions. He cannot blame anyone for the accidents that have happened to him, as for every bad situation on the road there is always a safe way out – we have to explore it for our own safety and for the safety of others. Avoiding an unsafe situation is always in our hands, knowingly no one ventures over them; provided of course we are aware. There are some flaws in the road design in certain locations and repeated accidents happen there. Blind curves, poor illumination, improper exit are some of the design aspects that may cause an accident.

Obstruction of visibility on the road is one of the most critical man made flaws of our system. Most of the corners are blocked up to the end of the road and a driver till he reaches up to the edge of the road, will not be able to see the traffic of other roads. This obstruction mostly develops there as a temporary structure and it can be addressed easily. The corner as such should be designed to give a safe visibility of cross roads – well before the driver actually reaches the edge of the road, at the junction.

Our many drivers don't differentiate between a junction and a regular straight stretch; and they keep the same speed in the junctions; this habit coupled with the visibility issue is one of the major reasons for accidents in our country.

All small or big junctions - anywhere this issue can be there and as a driver, one has to take precautions; and if visibility is not sufficient, they should simply slow down. Authorities should consider this as an opportunity for improvement. Many places on old roads, that have medians where drivers take a U turn; don't have a safe buffer zone on highways. Drivers are forced to stop in the fast lane and take a turn to the next fast lane; many accidents happen when other drivers come and hit them directly.

However, whatever may be the design faults on the roads; if a driver takes precautions he can prevent any accidents; only thing he has to take actions in advance. Many accidents happen when the driver makes a sudden decision in haste. He sees a U turn all of a sudden and takes turn; without bothering for the drivers behind or ahead.

All modern upcoming roads will not have these issues. Aim of this book is not to discuss any such issues, this book focuses on building a defensive driver in each driver occupying Indian roads and preparing them for the Road Revolution happening in our country.

CHAPTER TWO

ROLE OF THE DRIVING FORCE

In a train or a plane, two drivers and 2 pilots are there for safety reasons. On roads, where apart from vehicular traffic, pedestrians, animals, unsafe road conditions and many other unexpected hazards are there – a lone driver has to handle all the situations.

Driving is an art which every driver does in their own way and ultimately; the aim of remaining on the roads is to drive ensuring our own safety and safety of others - and to reach the destination in time. Like with other skills, the proficiency of an individual driver varies from person to person and hence his or her response for the same situation may not be similar to others.

Many more variables are also there among the drivers which alter their behaviour on roads and performance of vehicles. Age of driver and vehicle, mental status of driver, driving experience, type of load on the vehicle etc are some of the factors. Number of accidents will reduce drastically if all the drivers start behaving in the expected lines; which never happens.

Many near miss cases happen rampantly but never gets converted into an accident by timely corrective actions taken by one of the driver and this is a very important aspect of safe driving. As a driver; we not only should remain alert for our own safety, we also have to keep an eye on the mistakes of others to prevent an accident, to anticipate the movement of others.

Smooth movement of traffic is everybody's responsibility and therefore our actions should always be in the direction of ensuring that. A driver may find fault with another driver but he or she cannot do anything to correct them, so ignoring and moving ahead - is the best option on roads.

Most of the accidents gets averted if one of the drivers takes the correct step that normally a defensive driver takes. Our aim therefore should be to take the most appropriate steps in all the situations. It's true that all individuals are not likely to behave the same way; but if all know how to behave in a particular situation then safety on the road will have a different meaning.

One basic thing we all must not forget – Safety is a behavioural aspect and whatever efforts we put to train people about safety; unless they themselves accept and implement it by heart, individual's will still remain at risk. At the same time – a person without any formal knowledge or training of Safety, if asks one simple question in his mind before taking any action on roads, then his life will be secured – that is : What is the best possible solution in this situation?

Road safety is not a Rocket Science, all we have to do is to accept it as a, major threat - the society and all of us are now facing on roads. Then, automatically, all safe alternatives will be immediately, visible to us; on roads.

All the best solutions are already within us – we just have to explore it.

Our all accidents are pointing towards only one thing; we are behaving spontaneously without any thinking about a possible threat on the roads. Just a small restraint will prevent many accidents and awareness will completely eradicate this menace. This book is focussing on second part – but if all individual decides and behaves in most appropriate way, then this book is no longer required for the society.

The purpose of writing this book is to create a situation on the road for the driver and offer the best possible safe response. The contents of the books are not exhaustive and many more revisions may be needed to make it a near perfect reference handbook. The initiative is taken and it will evolve with time.

CHAPTER THREE

REALITY ON ROADS

We quiet often forget that even a normal speed can meet our needs.

Before we discuss anything about road safety in detail, we should know why avoiding an accident becomes our prime focus on our roads. We should understand one of the most important issue that we face on roads today. Many of the people who die in a road accident that happens today; can, in fact survive – if they get treatment in time; and this aspect should be our motivation to remain safe on road and avoiding an accident.

There is a golden hour of survival in any accident and if the patient is brought to the hospital in time or sometimes - if the victim is provided with first aid and then shifted; his chances of survival remains very high. This is generally of the order of one to one and half hour.

In road conditions most of the time this doesn't happen and getting an ambulance in time – reaching hospital in time all these things are not possible in remote areas. Sometimes others come to know about accident probably after many hours of the actual happening.

A patient brought to the medical facility within the Golden hour gives doctors an opportunity to revive them. First aid, if given in the site; increases the possibility of survival many times.

Unfortunately in our country a system for educating such first aid treatment to general public is not prevailing but cases are there when those trained have saved many lives. Even a person with no formal training can save a victim; we just have to step forward, what will we do if the victim is one among us – we will not leave them to their fate. Anything that will not complicate the case will definitely, will give some positive support to the victim. We have discussed about First Aid in details towards the end for this purpose.

General approach now is to call the ambulance and send the patient somehow to hospital and normally no one remains connected after that. If a proper follow up by the people who handle the patient immediately is done, then probably the patient may have a better chance of survival.

Few years back, while coming back from office, the author happen to see a crowd on road around a two wheeler accident victim, which happened around 10 – 12 minutes earlier.

The person was lying face down with apparently no movement, in a pool of blood. Cell phone videos were being made and information's were already sent for ambulance. Onlooker informed that the victim is dead and even police is informed. By just turning his face and opening his airways - he started breathing and later in hospital recovered too.

All latest vehicles are designed to withstand hardest possible impact on roads and have all the possible safety protections engineered to protect occupants – still, visuals of them ripping apart due to road accidents equally are dominating the news. No amount of design can protect one from death the way those vehicles are misused on roads – only a defensive driving practices within a driver's mind that is driving such vehicles can save.

Therefore in view of this scenario it becomes very important that the drivers who drive on the road should drive in such a way that, this type of unsafe situations does not arise.

Defensive driving is the best driving on the roads, which ensures safety of the self and those occupying roads, in any form. All the actions taken by a defensive driver are taken for this purpose only. No one is a born defensive driver and fortunately this skill can be acquired; all that is required is - a willingness to do so.

All new drivers, when they start moving on the roads independently, initially have some difficulty in moving smoothly and confidently. As time moves on, with more and more practice, this initial sluggishness disappears and they manoeuvre more fluidly.

In every driver's life different driving phases occur in sequence – initially the speed and charm of acquiring a new skill thrills them. They may like to show to others about their adventure, and here - their immaturity sometimes causes an accident. With a new driver; in this phase, many accidents happen, but many who overcome this phase safely - ultimately mature to become a defensive driver at a later stage of age.

However young people still remain prone to accidents and around 70% deaths are happening in the age group of 18 to 40 years.

Normally no one would wants to be involved in an accident, but this should not remain just in our wishful thinking; our all actions should speak about our - this intention. If you happen to see accident videos on YouTube; you will be surprised - the way drivers are simply throwing away their lives on the roads. It's really astonishing to see the way drivers behave, at times.

Roads are occupied by many types of vehicles 2-wheelers, 4 –wheelers (LMV & HMV) , extra wide bodied vehicles and extra-long vehicles. Car weighs around 1 ton and an empty truck itself weighs around 6 T and full truck around 30 Tons. Think about such heavy weight passing over our body parts, sometimes over the head itself. The pain caused by the impact of the high speed vehicle irrespective of its weight is unimaginable. Our body parts cannot withstand the impact; they are simply separated from our body.

But many really don't bothers about all such eventualities and simply drives carelessly. On our roads every day more than 430 deaths are happening and more than 4, 50,000 accidents happen per annum, in some or other place. Types of accidents are impact, overrunning, collision, overturning and reasons are over speeding, rash driving, not following rules, drinking & driving to illustrate a few.

Drivers who start as a rash driver ultimately may become a defensive driver with experience, age or after surviving from some accident. Our aim is not to waste time to create a defensive driver; but to train them as defensive driver before they actually start driving on roads.

Each driver has a right to know and understand the nuances of traffic hazards he is likely to encounter on the roads, before he actually starts driving on the roads. This book is created with a purpose, to bring down the rate of deaths in India; after observing that there is a repeated

pattern of accidents associated with particular reasons.

If a driver is equipped with that idea and already knows about the action he is required to take in those circumstances; then probably the accidents will have a downtrend. *We have to create a thinking mind with defensive driving software installed, in order to make our roads safer.* In this book we have done exactly this and brought out more than 55 reasons that are potential cause for almost 80% of the accidents.

Road accidents will not see the status of the person; there are many celebrities who perished on roads due to either the mistakes of their driver, or due to other vehicles or due to their own mistakes. In fact a rash driver can be dangerous to any one on the roads and training them is in the overall interest of the nation. A driver carrying a celebrity has more responsibilities; and he should behave in a completely defensive manner, while carrying them on road. As the presence of celebrity on the road, sometimes changes the dynamics of the road traffic.

Parents often recognise the accomplishments of their wards by presenting them with vehicles. There are many cases when such drivers drive at high speed in busy areas and cause major accidents. Parents should understand the need of educating the children about hazards involved on roads before gifting them such vehicles.

Those days were different, when vehicles were less in numbers and speed was less, traffic was fewer; now the things have changed. The vehicles are very powerful, speed is high, traffic on the road has gone up many times – we need to be careful for our own wards and for the safety of others. In many cases parents have lost their beloved ones in accidents or are fighting the legal battles, arising out of accidents.

CHAPTER FOUR

A DEFENSIVE DRIVER

Majority of the accidents are preventable – and only a driver can make it happen.

Defensive Driving is essentially driving in a manner that utilizes safe driving strategies, to enable motorists to address identified hazards; in a predictable manner.

Modern vehicles have all the gadgets provided, which help a driver to interpret & negotiate many scenarios on road for safety automatically and on our road still many older vehicles are there which don't have any such provisions.

A safe driver always believes his own eyes for taking any actions on road and apart from views in the mirrors, he will ensure that he is turning his neck and getting a very clear distinct view of the surroundings for taking any actions on roads. In pursuit of this, if he finds that he is unable to fetch the required view, he will slow down his speed and thus makes sure that he is not taking any risk.

He will always try to maintain an eye contact with the drivers in his vicinity for overall safety and to doubly ensure that they both are in harmony.

Defensive driving practices are actually the thinking that resides within the minds of each driver and guides them to tackle different situations on roads. They act proactively and reactively to guide the driver about the actions that need to be taken depending on the visuals seen by the eyes. All a driver has to do is to store the response for each type of situation in his mind and Defensive Driving Thinking will simply follow that and guide you to respond accordingly.

It is the responsibility of the individual to store the proper response in the mind and this can be easily learnt. This book is written with that purpose only and more than 50 situations are discussed in the book that are causing the majority of the accidents on roads. Accidents are happening due to the same reasons and out of ignorance many drivers are committing same mistakes again and again on the roads.

For each situation a connected thought is also brought out, so that as soon as we see a situation, a safe thought is automatically triggered in the mind.

CHAPTER FIVE

PEDESTRIAN SAFETY

Many accidents happen while pedestrians cross the road or just use the road normally for day to day work. More than 30, 000 pedestrians are dying per year in our country which is a whopping more than 20% of the total fatality in the country due to road accidents, and around 60,000 are injured with minor to critical injuries.

So while thinking about road accidents we should not think that only the drivers are involved, if our aim in the country is to reduce the death rate; we have to deal with it in totality. Whenever we are on roads, be it as a driver or simply as a pedestrian, a common road user; we all are governed by the road safety rules and should not occupy the roads casually.

Recently there were many accidents involving pedestrians when they were crossing the road at odd hours of the day when normally vehicles are less on the roads. Never assume that when there is no vehicles on the road, it is safe for a pedestrian to cross. In fact many of the drivers also consider such time as right time to drive the vehicles at high speed.

In the present cellphone age, distraction is the most common cause of accidents involving pedestrians on the roads. Tumbling on the road objects, missing the steps, suddenly coming in front of vehicles, casually walking in busy streets while talking on phone, all these visuals are now very common on the roads and of course causing many road accidents. Those who want to remain safe on the roads should very clearly make guidelines for their cellphone usage while they are occupying the roads. They should not venture any part of the road which they have not clearly surveyed with their eyes. Looking left and right and proceeding should be a life saving mantra lifelong for all of us, who have to use the same roads which is also used by other vehicles.

In addition to this we must understand the safety involved while crossing the roads. In our country though Zebra crossings are there in many roads but safety etiquettes involved with such crossing are not followed, by both drivers and pedestrians themselves. It is therefore very critically important that though as a pedestrian we should cross only from Zebra Crossing, wherever they are available; at the same time one should be very vigilant while crossing through them and always be prepared for a violation by a driver.

Which means there is not much difference between a Zebra crossing in Junctions, Zebra Crossing along the roads and an unauthorized road crossing anywhere in the road; as far as safety protocol to be followed by a pedestrian is concerned.

To understand the safety involved in our present road conditions where many high power, high speed vehicles are occupying the road, we must first understand the concept of distance traveled by a vehicle at different speeds in one second.

A vehicle traveling at 60 KM per hour travels 17 meters in 1 seconds. Similarly at 70 KM per hour the distance traveled is 19 m, for 80 – 22 m, 90 – 25 m, 100 – 28 m and 110 KM per hour it is 31 m. If the vehicle is traveling at 140 KM per hour it will cover 39 meters in 1 second.

Normally if we try to cross the road at a brisk pace we will take at least 6 seconds to cross the road. If it's a casual walk, it may take up to 10 seconds. Now assume we have decided to cross the road at a fast pace and started after ensuring no vehicle is there on the road by seeing Left and Right, which means it will take around 6 seconds of time for you to cross the road.

Now think of a situation where a speeding vehicle is coming towards you running at 100 KM per hour. When you started crossing the road; it was 168 meters (28 x 6) away from you and therefore was not visible to you, but still it will reach up to you by the time you cross the road. If the vehicle is running at 140 KM per hour, though it may be 235 meters away from you; which is more than the length of 2 football grounds - the vehicle can still reach up to you before you cross the road.

So when you start crossing the road after verifying and finding no vehicles around, never assume that no vehicle is going to come before you cross the road. Have a clear judgment of your expected time required to cross the road, cross promptly - don't rush. While crossing keep your eyes towards both sides, for any incoming vehicle, to remain safe during surprises mentioned above.

In a two way road, vehicle is expected from both the sides so have a clear view of both the sides of the road while crossing. In a one way road, on the first road you cross; a vehicle is normally coming from Right and on the second road, the vehicle will come from Left. But always expect surprises in our driving conditions.

Generally if a driver spots the pedestrian crossing the road during such situations, he tries to go from the back of the person. So if all of a sudden a vehicle appears on the road like this, try to continue the walk but still keep a close eye on the movement of the vehicle; as all drivers may not go from back. Never panic and create confusion; at that speed we have less than a second time to react - have a clear escape plan. If you know these things in advance there is no chance of any mishaps on the roads, crores of pedestrians are following this technique for their safety and only few are meeting wiht an accident due to ignorance.

If you are in a group and crossing from an unauthorized path, be sure that all are not going together - split the group and cross in small groups. Also make sure that while you are crossing a one way road never cross both the roads in ONE GO. Cross one road after following all safety norms, and for the second road again assess the safety and proceed.

Again while venturing out on roads during night, make sure that you are visible; by wearing light coloured clothes. From the driver point of view you must know that the driver who is able to see more than 1 KM during daytime, can see clearly only up to 600 meters during night, provided illumination is good. Visibility of the driver also comes down rapidly if the speed is more, higher the speed narrower the visibility.

We must also remember that the driver will invariably try to save us if he is able to spot us on the roads. In that situation the driver will deflect the vehicle and sometimes that may become another accident. Many major accidents are happening in the country while the drivers are attempting to save the pedestrians.

As a pedestrian we are also responsible to make sure that we are not creating any unsafe situation for others by our presence. We are visible to drivers on road and we are also aware of all the aspects of road safety is very important. Ignorance can not be an excuse after an accident it happens on the road. We also must understand that in the event of a collision with a vehicle we only are going to get severely injured or killed. All our actions on roads should be safe for us and for other road occupants too.

In general there are no separate pedestrian crossing lights in most of the cities. Pedestrians are expected to make their own safety by observation and so while on the road be a keen observer and remain aware.

So far we have discussed safety involved in walking across the roads, another most important aspect of walking along the road is WALKING FROM RIGHT.

While walking along the roads for day to day work, going to school, for morning walks etc. many accidents happen when the vehicles from behind comes and hit the pedestrians; catching them - Unaware.

Such accidents happen only due to the fact that the pedestrians are not able to see the vehicle coming. In most of such cases the driver never does it intentionally, but his fails to control the vehicle in certain circumstances (these situations are discussed in this book in other chapters). Since the vehicle is coming from behind, the pedestrian is not able to see the vehicle and thus is not able to take any actions to save themselves. These accidents can be avoided if we make a practice of walking from the Right Side of the road. Vehicle move from left side of the road, you walk from the right side, against the flow of the vehicle direction.

Which means if you are walking on a Two Way Road where vehicles move in both directions, you will be walking on the right side of the road along your direction of walk like the picture below.

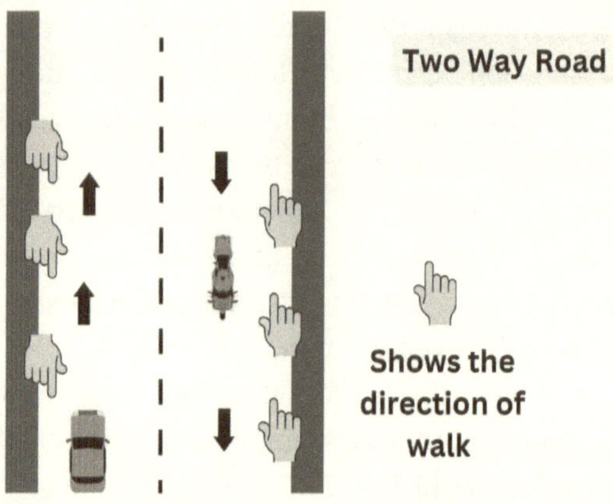

While walking on a One Way Road where vehicles move only in one direction you will be walking on the Right Side of the road in the direction of your walk, like this.

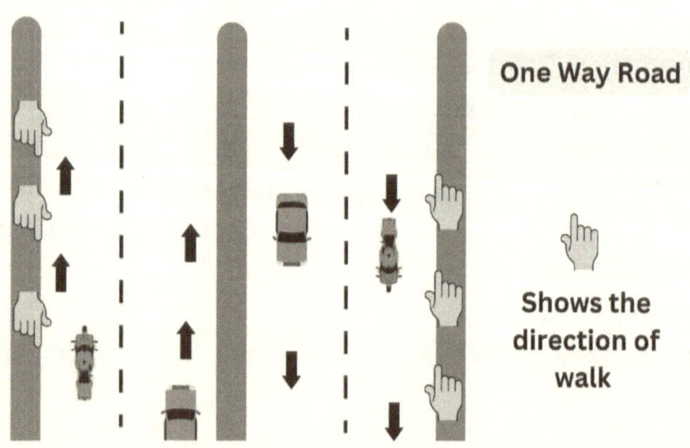

Advantages of walking on the right side of the road is you will be continuously facing the incoming vehicles and will be able to see them coming in front of you. Additionally four eyes, two of the pedestrian and two of the driver now monitor the safety; chances of an accident comes down considerably.

This complete book basically focuses on the drivers, their behavior and safety - but as a pedestrian all of us are expected to know about the hazards involved in driving to remain safe on the road, which involves all the aspects of driving safety too.

CHAPTER SIX

BE YOUR OWN SAFEST DRIVER

Defensive Thinking No 1 : I am the most important person in the universe and all my actions taken on the road, will be to safeguard me from an accident. Due to my actions, the safety of others will never be endangered on roads.

You are too precious to someone in this world and don't deserve to involve in an accident on roads, due to your own mistake or that of others.

On road the safety begins with us; and while on roads, all should keep this important aspect in mind. All individuals; irrespective of their hierarchical level in the society - are important. They are loved ones for their family, may be children for them or parents. Never forget you are important for the society itself; due to the contribution you are making in some form or other, to the nation – all are precious and someone is always waiting for you, somewhere.

While driving consider that you are carrying the most important person in the universe in your vehicle – and no one can deny this fact: you indeed are most precious to yourself and to someone. It is your primary duty to protect this person in the overall interest of the universe at any cost - and this you have to do for that special person, who is waiting for you. Many, who are in the autumn years of their life, definitely might have come across a situation in their early years of life; when an accident could have changed their fate altogether; but for their safe action on the road - that day.

Every day we lose more than 430 people on roads, today while you are reading this book ; 430 citizens of this country will not come back home, alive. Just think; if they somehow could avoid this fate to their life; the journey would have been entirely different for many today. A driver should always have thinking for their own safety; our all actions on roads will change automatically - if this very understanding of road safety comes in our mind.

You play different roles as drivers on roads; sometime you carry yourself, sometimes your beloved ones, friend or at times a group of people, or a dignitary – a celebrity. On all these occasions your mind-set may be different - sometimes joyful, thrilled, or even tense and in hurry. Take any road accident, that happens around; mostly have a reasons attributable to driver's mistakes and if any accident could have been averted on roads; only the drivers must have made it happen.

If such is the importance of driving and with so many precious lives involved, why a driver on roads; sometimes make very basic mistakes, is beyond our imagination. A driver can be seen just venturing in any small gap available on roads without any second thought. In fact a driver should not think even an inch beyond his actual visibility on roads. He should always consider the safety of his all immediate next moves – after all it may sometimes cost him, his own life.

Many youngsters can be seen on roads carrying pillion riders very dangerously, in an act of rash driving. The driver must ask those pillion riders – they definitely must be scared. We have seen many act of such rash driving simply ending dangerously; taking away lives of many other innocent road users along with them. After accidents in such situations, if the driver survives; instances are there, where they got thrashing from people around. A driver should never become a threat for himself and others.

Unfortunately in social media such type of videos are getting good patronages and audience are watching these videos regularly and that shows, our approach and sensitivity towards road safety.

Everyone may not be privileged to have a driver, but all drivers are definitely drivers for themselves. **So if you are safe - all are safe.**

As a driver or rider you are not performing an ordinary task; at stake are many precious lives, including yours – THE MOST IMPORTANT PERSON IN THE UNIVERSE. **You will not and should not; put yourself in danger.** This thinking in mind alone will bring lot of changes in the behaviours of the drivers on the road.

CHAPTER SEVEN

CONSIDERATION FOR OTHERS.

Defensive Thinking No 2 : I will always have consideration for others on the road and I will always respect the right of way of others on the road. My actions on the roads will always enhance road safety for me and others.

If we were to make the conscious and frequent effort of treating others with consideration, the effects on us and on society as a whole would be amazing."

- Henry Charles Link

As we have already told; driving skill varies from person to person and we really cannot do anything to correct the person there on the roads, we are together only for a few seconds on roads. So the best possible preparation on road is to expect that you will always come across drivers who may not be as perfect as you, and drive considering this fact.

While on the road, always have consideration for others. On the road everyone needs a safe space to move around and it is the responsibility of all other drivers to provide the driver, with that space. A defensive driver will always ensure that his vehicles are safely away from other vehicles. For this he will have clear judgement of his own vehicle's length and width; particularly the corners of vehicle; which is not visible to him directly.

In slow moving traffic around the junctions, when bumper to bumper movement happens; we have to be very careful not to touch other vehicles. Our speed should be such that we are not hitting the front vehicle, at the same time our braking requirement should not force the rear vehicle to hit us.

On roads this is most common accident, someone will stop suddenly and the person behind will be forced to stop too. Who may stop after bumping on the vehicle ahead or not; depends upon his style of driving, but the third person behind him will come and crash on him. This situation can come in junctions where speed may be reasonably slow or in a freeway at high speed. If you have consideration for others; drive in such a fashion that because of your driving, such situations should not happen to others. Have a clear plan of your speed and maintain required distance between vehicles without fail. If you find that the person behind you is not maintaining the safe gap in speed zone, without much delay in a planned way allow him to go ahead; you will be safe.

In slow speeds, driver tend to take things casually and sometime take their eyes off the roads – distraction of a fraction of second can be fatal occasionally.

The moment someone considers **"Concern for Others"** as the prime responsibility of the defensive driver; many of the accident causing situations automatically disappears. Now the driver knows the importance of not indulging in over speeding, maintaining the gaps, maintaining mirrors, effective brakes, healthy indication lights, and the need for dimming the lights – all these support him in his pursuit for consideration for others.

If you see from your own end, about what are your expectations on the road; definitely getting a driver who has concern for you – it's just give and take. Many of our accidents are happening as we miss this important aspect of driving.

Sometimes, a driver fails to give side for overtaking to someone due to some traffic situation; there are instances where they followed that driver and hit his vehicle with stones in the next junction.

Peace of mind is the most important thing in driving; it affects both the parties, if its missing. To drive safely on roads we have to keep our cool and as per traffic situation and your own driving capabilities - always yield way to others, if you think anyhow you cannot go faster than that. If really the situation is as per your assessment only, the person who was blaring horn from behind, after sometime you will find - comes in front. **Always yield to the right of way to others; if they deserve.**

ON a two way road; each half of the road is fixed for **to and fro** moving traffic. For all normal movement of traffic the drivers are required to remain in their LEFT side only. There may be a partition marking line or may not be there; yet a driver should create an imaginary line in their mind and stick to their half only. When a need for overtaking a vehicle comes; the driver should ensure that no vehicle is coming from opposite side and then only should move for overtaking. Even if one vehicle is coming it is a violation if you cross your half, and in curves no one should overtake in a two way road. In this situation many accidents are happening on our roads. Many accidents happen when the driver cosses the line for overtaking without properly seeing vehicles coming from opposite side or behind; few seconds of delay is always worth waiting on roads.

On roads, we can find drivers; who - when someone tries to overtake them, increases their speed and don't allow those drivers to have a safe overtaking.

Never get involved in any argument with any one on roads, even if you are correct – you may probably win that argument; but as a driver you may fail in your further journey somewhere! sometimes!

Just have concern for others in your mind and driving on the road will automatically become smooth for you. All may not believe in it and for many this may be a laughing stuff also – but those who believe in it, strongly experience it on the roads.

CHAPTER EIGHT

WHY A TIRE BURST?

There are many reasons and situations for a tyre burst to happen, and as a driver we all must know them. Tyre, in fact, plays the most important role in the safe journey of any vehicle and passengers. Unfortunately, most of the drivers are not aware about the safety associated with tyres.

We will be discussing some major factors that affect the life of any vehicle and directly the safety of the vehicle along with occupants.

Proper Recommended tyre, with right installation.

It is important that installed tyre in a vehicle is of same size as recommended by the vehicle manufacture. Each tyre has different patterns, size and loading capacity which also differs across brands. Mixing different tyre technologies and construction techniques of different brands disturbs the entire balance and performance between the four tyres and negatively impact the lives of all four tyres.

Wear and tear of the tyres will not be even, if balancing and alignment of the tyres installed are not correct. A wrongly balanced vehicle wheel will have uneven wear and tear of the wheel and it may damage a wheel prematurely. Always consult the professional for this important aspect of the vehicle safety and never compromise in quality while replacing the tyres.

Periodically the all wheels need to be rotated between front and back, to have even wear and tear in all the wheels.

Tyre Pressure

The weight of the load is carried by the air within the tyre, not by the tyre itself. Maintaining the correct inflation pressure is absolutely necessary to guarantee the tyre's performance. Pressure should always be set to, and maintained at the maximum load pressure specification recommended by the tyre manufacturer.

- Underinflating causes excessive deflection in the tyre, increasing the heat level and leading to premature tyre failure.
- Overinflating restricts the natural deflection of the tyre, which also leads to premature tyre failure.

Both under-pressure and overpressure are detrimental to the life of a tyre. If the inflation in the tyre is low; the under-pressure increases the radial deformation of the tyre and damages both the sidewalls of the tyre faster. This increases the tread and shoulders wear and increases the temperature of the tyre to abnormally high. Heat is the biggest enemy of a rubber tyre, which very rapidly deteriorates the life of the tyre.

Many drivers have a misconception that over-pressure in the tyre is good to carry heavier goods. High tyre pressure increases the tyre rigidity and deformation, which also leads to the reduced contact area on the road. This aggravates the central tread wear and reduces the comfort of driving and life of the tyre as well. With just 25% of increase in pressure the tyre life is reduced by about 30%.

Heat build up

Heat is the tyre's worst enemy and is caused by several factors. As a tyre rotates under the weight of a vehicle and its load, it repeatedly deforms and recovers, which generates lots of energy. When this energy is released, heat builds up, making it more susceptible to wear, cuts and structural fatigue. The amount of heat build-up is determined by several factors including, Underinflation, Overloading, High speeds and harsh braking, Aggressive cornering, poorly designed or badly maintained roads, Working outside tyre specs, Seasonal influences etc.

All tyres are designed to carry a maximum permitted load and maximum designed speed. These details are embedded on the tyre along with other details. Loading tyres beyond the permitted load and over speeding beyond the rates speed also causes the tyres to fail prematurely. Picture below indicates the details of the permitted load and speed codes used in tyres.

LOAD INDEX & SPEED RATING
LOAD INDEX
SPEED RATING
235 / 55 R17 99W
99w, 99 is load
index & W is
speed limit

Speed Index	Max Speed
N	140
P	150
Q	160
R	170
S	180
T	190
U	200
H	210
V	240
Z	240+
W	270
Y	300

Load Index & Max Speed Index (KM/ Hr)

Load Index of tyres					
Load Index	Load Per Tyre (Kg)	Load Index	Load Per Tyre (Kg)	Load Index	Load Per Tyre (Kg)
62	265	87	545	112	1120
63	272	88	560	113	1150
64	280	89	580	114	1180
65	290	90	600	115	1215
66	300	91	615	116	1250
67	307	92	630	117	1285
68	315	93	650	118	1320
69	325	94	670	119	1360
70	335	95	690	120	1400
71	345	96	710	121	1450
72	355	97	730	122	1500
73	365	98	750	123	1550
74	375	99	775	124	1600
75	387	100	800	125	1650
76	400	101	825	126	1700
77	412	102	850	127	1750
78	435	103	875	128	1800
79	437	104	900	129	1850
80	450	105	925	130	1900
81	462	106	950	131	1950
82	475	107	975	132	2000
83	487	108	1000	133	2060
84	500	109	1030	134	2120
85	515	110	1060	135	2180
86	530	111	1090	136	2240

Tire Shelf Life

Most important aspect of tyre safety is its shelf life or number of years it was used after manufacturing. All tyre manufactures and safety group associated with Road Safety recommend a tyre replacement after roughly 5-6 years of usage. This is confirmed by the European Tyre and Rim Technical Organisation (ETRTO), which states that tyres may be considered safe and new for 5 years from the date of manufacture.

The tyre manufacturing date is a four-digit code embedded on the tyre's sidewall. The first two digits represents the week of manufacture, while the last two digits indicates the last two digit of the year of manufacture. For instance, if the code is "2218," it indicates that the tyre was manufactured in the 22nd week of 2018. Please refer the picture below for clarity in the manufacturing details.

22, Indicates 22nd Week of the year.

18, Indicates the year 2018

With age, the rubber compounds tend to harden, which affects the performance of the tyres, even if it is not used much.

Driving Habits

Tyre burst can happen due to various reasons as mentioned above but our own driving habit also plays a very important road in that. Not all person drives the same way. The way you treat your vehicle has a direct impact on it and its parts. Starting the vehicle in a fast mode, emergency braking, sharp steering, driving in high speed even on bad roads, hitting regularly against curbs and parking barriers are just a few of driving habits that eat away the life of the tyre.

Many tyre bursts happen when drivers try to overtake a vehicle in high speed. When sudden direction change happens in the vehicle at high speed, it is the tyre that experience all the force of the change in direction with load. Any weak point in tyre at that moment of time may fail and a tyre burst can happen.

How to avoid a tire burst

1. To avoid a tyre failure while driving we need to regularly monitor the tyre for any crack or damage in the treads. Age of the tyre should be monitored and tyre should be changed irrespective of the good conditions of the tyre after 6 years.
2. Periodically do the balancing and rotation of tyres to have even wear and tear of the wheels.

3. Regular air check, preferably Nitrogen to be used in the tyre and rated pressure should be maintained. Long distance traveling invariably increases the pressure. If the tyres are filled up to rated pressure, increase in pressure will be within the limits only. Air filled using a portable pressure gauge in a road side shop may be incorrect and it should be avoided. Digital trusted petrol pump air filling system should be used for safety.

4. Overloading, over speeding, rash driving and sudden change in direction should be avoided every time. These are very well-known situations when tyre bursts have happened on roads.

5. While driving you should predict the driving conditions in advance and drive in such a way that a sudden braking situation should not arise at all.

6. Abrupt overtaking should be avoided and it should be done gradually in a planned manner.

CHAPTER NINE

Junctions and Crossovers

If you want to be safe everywhere, then the most important step is to monitor your behaviour at Junctions and Crossovers.

Never cross the junctions at high speeds

Defensive Thinking No 3 : A Junction is coming ahead, I must slow down gradually and after ensuring all round safety, then only I must cross the junction.

Junctions are the area where most of the accidents happen in our country. After analysing the reasons; the facts emerged are clearly indicating that - drivers are not slowing down in junctions and if it is a junction without signals then many are not following the rules. In a junction with traffic police and signals, speeding while crossing the junction and flouting of rules by escaping the eyes of traffic police is a major cause for accidents.

A defensive driver invariably slows down in a junction to a safe speed; slowing down does not mean an abrupt slowing. There are many indicators provided on the road to tell a driver about the incoming cross road or junction; like sign boards or rumble strips. As soon as a defensive drive observes a junction ahead; he immediately takes necessary corrective actions and crosses the junction following all safety norms and traffic signal.

There are many junctions; where there will not be any lights and traffic police posting; in such types of junctions it is the responsibility of the individual driver to ensure safety and proceed. In all such areas a safe driver slows down; looks left and right and proceeds after ensuring the safety. It should just get planted in the mind of the driver to be vigilant in a junction road. This one aspect is so important in our country that; if everyone starts practising this safety rule, then around 30% of the accidents will vanish from our roads.

In fact slowing down at a junction slightly ahead of actually reaching the junction, enhances the safety of the road in a big way. This way a driver can control the speed of the vehicle behind. There are many accidents involving the back vehicle bumping on to the vehicles ahead; when a signal or any other safety requirement forces the driver ahead to stop. Vehicles behind will always try to force the vehicle ahead to move continuously on our roads and it's our duty to keep this safety aspect in mind. In juctions by slowing down slightly in advance and on highways by giving them side to go ahead.

In a junction always you can expect a surprise like the person ahead suddenly applying brake; suddenly one person decides to take a turn, a pedestrian - an animal also can cross your line and which may force you to apply brake and person behind may bump on you. Keep the speed between 20 - 30 KM/Hr and never take your eye off the roads while crossing junctions.

In fact, while moving on a road, particularly when you are passing through a busy two-way road, where both side shops or houses are there; whenever you come across even a small junction - moving slowly is the best option that one driver should opt for. Any surprises coming from that small road, will force you to either apply brakes or suddenly take a turn to avoid an accident, because you will always try to save that person or vehicle – in both situations, the driver coming straight is in trouble – that's you.

Crossing the junction at a safe speed is always ensures overall safety.

No traffic time, lean traffic time, early hours, late night when no one is around - drivers tend to move and cross junctions at very fast speed assuming or even after actually seeing no vehicle around. Unfortunately this is the time we have more accidents on our road.

Never forget our junctions are not made as per norms, most of the junction will not have proper cross visibility. Sometimes, to beautify the junction ; we provide fencing and do plantation - which makes it very difficult for all to see each other.

Junction is the place where all flexi banners are put by many and they simply block your visibility. Big- big banners just at the corners – gross violation of the safety norm – but this is the reality.

We know in one second a vehicle can travel 22 meters, if it is running at 80 KM/Hr speed. Speed – blind views; all these make it very difficult for you to see the other drivers or vehicles when you cross the junction area, in less than 1 second; an accident is bound to happen.

So whatever may be the time of the day, traffic is there or not – risk is always there – move slowly and cautiously through junctions, have a clear view of the surrounding and cross.

Never jump the signals

Defensive Thinking No 4 : I will follow all the traffic signals and in the junction even if the signals are not there, I will take all my precautions of slowing down, Looking Left and Right and then only I will proceed.

Better late than DEAD on TIME

Traffic signals are provided to regulate the movement of vehicles so that safety on roads is ensured. Unfortunately many of our accidents happen at such traffic signal junctions only. Impatience of drivers on the road is the major cause for such accidents – followed by rule violation by the drivers; they follow rules - if someone is monitoring them.

Few years back we happened to be driving on a highway in a foreign country during late 11 o'clock in the night – signals were still in operation and almost zero traffic was there. In a RED signal, a lone bike rider was seen patiently waiting for signal to get green; surveillance cameras may also be the reason for such behaviour but such drivers are there right here in our country too.

A defensive driver obeys the rule not for the sake of compliance but for ensuring the safety on roads.

Starting vehicles instantaneously when signal becomes Green or even before and not stopping On RED

Defensive Thinking No 5 : I will not start immediately after the signals are becoming GREEN and I will not cross the junction after the signal has gone RED.

Road safety is a state of mind; accident is an absence of mind

In our road conditions, many drivers don't stop immediately after the Red signal, some still try to pass through, assuming to clear before the arrival of drivers from the next Green sequence. This calculation goes awry when the driver of the next green signal starts instantaneously or a little early.

There are times when traffic may be lean; late in the evening, early morning afternoon hours. Anytime when the traffic is lean many drivers assume that they can jump RED and still can manage. Normally when the signals are in operation, general tendency for most of the driver is to follow it totally. Whenever such drivers take occasional risks; others are usually caught unaware and they suddenly find this violator in their path. You can find many drivers trying to clear against the traffic flow at times, creating very unsafe scary situation for others and sometimes horrible accidents – because behind them already a steady flow of traffic will be there; which will overrun them.

A defensive driver will stop if he is expecting a Red Signal before he crosses the line, in a planned way; and while starting on Green Signal - will take stock of the situation around him and then start at a slow safe speed.

Crossing the Junction after the Amber or Yellow signal

Defensive Thinking No 6 : I should never forget that the Amber or Yellow is a Warning Sign and if the signal is Yellow - I will slow down and will stop before the line.

Reaching your destination is a reward for safe driving

Many drivers encountering an Amber or Yellow light at junctions or cross roads, tend to increase the speed and try to cross the junction in a hurry. Many drivers from far off distance when they see Yellow, start honking horns to force the driver ahead to cross the junction. All of us mostly forget to consider Yellow as a signal to slow down and stop.

A defensive driver will slow down immediately after seeing a Yellow and safely stop the vehicle at line. If it so happens that it becomes Yellow after he almost reached the line – then he will consider moving ahead but at a controlled speed. If a timer is there in the Junction which tells about the remaining time then decision making becomes easy.

Invariably however a defensive drive will slightly slow down to a safe speed upon seeing a junction and always cross the junction safely. A slower speed always alleviates the possibility of an accidents and helps in taking safe proactive actions.

Follow rules only when someone is around to monitor.

Defensive Thinking No 7 : I will always abide by the rules, whether a traffic authority is there to monitor or not.

"You don't need to know the whole alphabet of Safety. The A, B, C of it will save you if you follow it: Always Be Careful."
– Colorado School of Mines Magazine

Traffic rules are to be adhered; by every driver, and all occupants of road - under all circumstances; irrespective of, if there is a traffic authority around or not. All the drivers are expected to follow it and all drivers also expect that the other drivers will follow it too. And under this situation if a driver fails to observe rules - it creates an unsafe situation for all others.

Just think a situation, tomorrow authorities decide and install surveillance cameras on all potential locations and start imposing penalties to all violators with proof. Whether the situation will remain same or a change will start immediately, in the behaviours of each driver.

A defensive driver follows the traffic signal rule not for compliance sake, but because he himself wants that the roads of their country should be safe and the number of accidents should be less and this aspect of maintaining discipline, remains his prime contribution towards that. Assume a camera is monitoring all our behaviours on road every time and act accordingly.

Place yourself in correct location

Defensive Thinking No 8 : I will plan my next turn in advance and place myself correctly in a junction for smooth turning

"Carefulness costs you nothing. Carelessness may cost you your life."– Safety saying

After the signal turns green in a traffic junction, many drivers start moving - from leftmost side to right side of road; across the flow of traffic to take a right turn. This planning, a safe driver does in advance and places himself accordingly; so that flow of the traffic is not affected and he is able to turn safely.

Overtaking inside a junction

Defensive Thinking No 9 : I will never overtake inside a junction and I will wait and after crossing the junction only I will overtake.

Prepare and prevent, don't repair and repent."

– Author unknown

Overtaking inside a junction is the deadliest action of the drivers on roads. The vehicle which the driver overtakes becomes a blind spot for himself and for the driver coming from the opposite direction in the right angle. Your visibility will be blocked because of the very vehicle you are overtaking. There are hundreds of accidents happening on roads due to this reason and it should be known to one and all. YouTube is full of such videos where a driver can be seen simply getting a direct impact from the other direction vehicle, subsequently the vehicle he tried to overtake; itself, sometimes overruns him.

You can even find drivers overtaking within the junction when the signal is Red and causing major accidents – three violation; one, over speeding in junction and second, overtaking within junction - third, when the signal is RED. Very important things and a drive should observe them very seriously.

OVER SPEEDING – THE KILLER NO 1

Speed thrills but kills.

Defensive Thinking No 10 : I will never overspeed and keep my speed according to road conditions.

Speed is a killer number one on the roads, youngsters are mostly getting trapped - in this ***thrill to nowhere.*** It is very easy to increase the speed by twisting the accelerator; but on the road the most important safety rule is how efficiently and safely you are able to come to a halt in an eventuality.

All modern vehicles are designed to stop safely whenever a situation demands. Standard testing conditions under which these vehicles are tested is entirely different from ground reality on roads. On roads the surface may be slippery, at times sand or dust may be there on the road – which will not give you any grip on roads, any stray animal or a kid may suddenly appear in front; giving you no time to respond.

Defensive drivers apart from following the traffic guidelines; will also consider factors like how efficiently they will be able to control the vehicle, condition of the tyres, types of brakes available in the vehicle (drum, disc or ABS) , road condition , traffic on roads, school area , hospital area, clear visibility in front of him – there are many factors that will decide your safe speed.

You will find many accidents involving drivers crashing directly onto the vehicle ahead, whenever the person in front suddenly applies brakes. This is because of two reasons, one the driver is not maintaining the required safe distance and second the speed is much more than stipulated in that situation. There may not be a board indicating the stipulated speed, but the safe driver always analyses the surroundings and decides the safe speed. These are very basic precautions one has to take on the roads as a driver; at the same time these types of accidents are very common on our roads, which indicates that the fundamental discipline and understanding of driving itself is lacking in many of the drivers.

We have to monitor our driving pattern and if you are forced to apply brakes more often, then consider you are driving faster than required. If you are required to frequently change the lane to maintain your speed – you are driving faster and you are at risk. A defensive driver need not frequently apply brakes and change the lane – it clearly indicates an aggressive driving tendency, which is a dangerous sign.

Before driving at a fast speed, one should clearly understand the Response time, Reaction time and Braking time in the process of actual Braking of a vehicle. When we see an obstruction on the road through your eyes, where we need to apply a sudden brake; we process this signal in our mind and decide to apply the brake. The time taken from seeing the obstruction to taking a decision to apply brakes is our response time and it is normally of the order of 1 second.

After we decide , we react and apply brakes - this time is called reaction time and here we physically apply brake. Actual stoppage of the vehicle actually happens after this only and this time is the braking time. The vehicle stops after completion of response, reaction and braking time. And during this entire period the vehicle is continuously moving; for the first 1 second at the same speed at which it was running and subsequently gradually at a reducing speed before coming to halt.

Distance traveled also depends on whether the road surface is dry or wet. For 80 KM/ hr on dry surface a 4 wheeler vehicle will stop after traveling around 69 meters and if the surface is wet then it will stop after 85 meters. Similarly for 90 KM/ hr these figures are 83 & 103, for 100 KM/hr 98 & 122 and for 110 KM/hr they are 113 & 143 meters. These figures are self-explanatory and reveal the dangers involved with high-speed driving.

If the vehicle has to travel this far before actually coming to halt; chances of a driver or the other party escaping the collision is very less. This problem is further complicated if this situation arises in a curved road as in that situation a driver has to additionally tackle a slip and skid also.

Also in an accident, the severities of the injuries are manifold if it happens at high speed. Since our aim is to avoid an accident altogether, the best possible prevention is to control the speed. At one point of high speed, even there is no requirement of an obstruction for an accident to happen; the driver themselves loses the control of the vehicle; due to inertia of the vehicle.

If you see the racing tracks, where you officially can ride the bike or drive the car at maximum possible speed of the machine, the situation is entirely different. There the protection gears they wear are designed to protect them in the worst possible crashes. Youngsters, who do the same in a normal road, without wearing even a basic protection of Crash Helmet, after they get motivated seeing such actions in race tracks and movies, must clearly understand that those people are trained and are professional.

Conditions on race tracks are absolutely safe and those roads will not have any obstructions, other than competitors. If they skid on the tracks not a single part of their body will actually touch the ground, they are so covered and protected with safety gears.

In movies most of the stunts are produced in studios may be through a duplicate professional, a character of the movie sometimes need not drive a vehicle actually. We should not emulate them just like that and risk our lives and that of others on roads.

A safe and defensive driver normally never finds a reason to apply a sudden brake on the road. He observes the traffic flow around him very closely and takes appropriate corrective actions in his speed and gap between vehicles - in a proactive manner well in advance. **Therefore a safe speed for a vehicle is the speed which is within the speed limit in the zone, which gives full control to the driver and he or she is in a position to safely maneuver around and is around the average speed of the vicinity.**

Apart from the Speed Limit, every stretch of the road has an average speed which varies depending on many conditions; like, number of vehicles, time of the day, climatic condition, school or office time. A driver should set their speed accordingly.

Many times it comes to our mind; what distance between two vehicles is a safe distance; if you are trailing and following a vehicle. If you are at a lower speed below 60, then the distance traveled by your vehicle in 3 seconds is the minimum distance requirement and for higher speed 80 and above; it should be 6 seconds. For information, a vehicle traveling at 60 KM per hour travels 17 meters in 1 seconds. Similarly at 70 the distance traveled is 19 m, 80 – 22 m, 90 – 25 m, 100 – 28 m and 110 KM per hour it is 31 m.

Many drivers indulge in Tail gating, means driving at high speed just behind a moving vehicle and waiting for an opportunity to overtake. Sometimes due to some situation in front of the vehicle ahead, that vehicle driver may apply brake, a major accident will happen. Even if the driver manages to overtake, his focus will be in speed and maintaining the gap and while doing so he may commit some fatal mistakes. Never do Tail Gating behind a vehicle. If you happen to be the driver who is driving the vehicle in front; always allow such drivers to overtake you safely. It will just avoid an unsafe situation for both you and the driver Tail Gating You.

Controlling your speed and your chances of hitting other vehicles head on will never exist. A safe speed not only reduces the chance of an accident; but it also gives you an opportunity to react and take actions to save yourself.

In curved roads if you resort to over speeding, then, your chances of skidding while negotiating the curves and jumping to other vehicle's paths also increases. Many accidents happen when the drivers don't reduce the speed in curves and due to high speed fail to turn along with the curve due to centrifugal force and hit the barricade or cross to other road or go inside a vehicle. Many accidents happen on curved roads and ghat roads where a driver misses their judgment and falls into ditches.

In curves, without fail a driver must reduce the speed. Sometimes in curves a junction also may be there; these two make a deadly combination on roads.

Many accidents are happening when the driver reaches a junction at high speed and takes a sudden turn. In this situation the chances of overshooting the junction becomes very high. Other drivers coming straight will not be expecting a sudden vehicle turning like this. Normally a driver is expected to slow down, wait, take stock of the situation and proceed or turn.

Taking a right angle turn (both in left or right direction) or passing through a roundabout at high speed are the situations where the vehicles are toppling on the roads. Here the drivers should understand the science behind the centrifugal force, which throws them outwards in the curvatures. There may be many factors in addition to speed which will add to this force - like loose items carried by them; sand, bricks, water, animals, people, anything that can also move away while turning, throws the vehicle outside.

Whoever is planning to take a turn in the junction must understand this and should slow down well before reaching the junction and take turns at a lower speed after ensuring safety in the junctions.

However all drivers while approaching junction from any side; should always expect a surprise at the junctions and adjust their speed to meet such eventualities. Junctions are the areas where in our road conditions - things don't happen in the normal way, there will always be a clash between the thinkings of different drivers.

A defensive driver will always keep a window for the mistakes of others. Never forget that though the mistake may be from the other driver's side; but the life at stake

is of you and your family also. As we have mentioned earlier; in our road junctions, visibility as such will not be proper due to poor design and if the other driver suddenly appears before you like this - it may not be possible for you to spot them in advance.

Invariably, a safe driver should maintain a safe corridor of visibility in front of them, for safety and ensuring safe response in eventuality. As brought out earlier, a vehicle traveling at speed more than 100 KM/hr can be safely stopped only after a distance of around 100 meters, which is almost equal to the length of a football field. Such a long distance for safely stopping a vehicle can be found in a Runway only when no planes are around.

In our road conditions 100 KM/ hour is a very unsafe speed, and if a driver is driving at this speed or beyond, then they definitely must ensure a safe clear - straight - unhindered visibility up to 150 meters in front of them. For every 10 KM/hr speed extra 30 meters distance should be considered.

Since dynamics of the road changes every 10 meters, no assumptions about visibility should be made on roads. Depending on what you are actually able to see clearly only, a driver should take the decision.

Due to any reasons if the visibility is falling below these distances, reducing the speed to a safe speed is the only option. As a norm one should keep distance traveled by the vehicle in 6 seconds as a safe distance.

Reasons for poor visibility or failure of distance judgment may be many, curved road, overtaking distractions, distraction of phones, foggy weather, rains, darkness etc; but a driver should never forget to bring down the speed to safe zone, as soon as they sense a problem with visibility.

Any time if the driver senses that any of their next stretch is going to be blind for them, means they will reach that location physically, without actually seeing it in advance with their eyes - it should be considered as a danger and such situations should be negotiated in low speed only.

One of the major reasons for high speed accidents is that most of our drivers negotiate the obstructions just by changing the direction. We always tend to forget that brakes are also provided in the vehicle, instead of reducing the speed using accelerator and brakes; most prefer to change direction. The only option is to control the speed , you will remain in the safe known zone - if you change the direction without reducing the speed; your chances of an unsafe - unknown zone, coming in front will be more. This becomes very dangerous if you overtake at high speed and suddenly find some obstruction or a vehicle. Overtaking from the wrong left side at high speed is very dangerous as you are going to the edge of the road.

Sometimes on roads, the drivers indulge in racing - naturally now the concentration would be more on the racing and this situation creates an unsafe environment on the road. There is a lot of difference between a normal road and a racing track, where all the vehicles are involved for the same purpose. But on normal roads all other vehicles are running at normal safe speed following all the safety rules. All of a sudden this speeding vehicle appears around them, catches them unaware and an accident may happen. Sometimes people sitting inside a vehicle only decide for a race to set some record speed and they may violate all norms to achieve that, resulting in an accident for them or innocents around. While driving or riding only safety should be there in our thinking. All other thoughts are dangerous while you are driving.

In modern vehicles the suspension system and steering arrangements are so advanced that people sitting inside may not realize at what speed they are driving, unless they monitor the speedometer; it's so smooth. Since all the windows are closed they won't be listening to the traffic noise and wind sound - they simply can not realize when the vehicle crosses 100. These vehicles are designed to run at 200 or more; but the question is - are our roads designed for that or can our drivers control the vehicle at that speed on general road conditions. Anything can happen on our roads, all other vehicles are running at speed varying from 40 to 100, a slow driver may be occupying the fast lane, a pothole or a hump on bridge, an animal, or even sometimes due to unforseen situations, on a one way - you can suddenly find vehicles coming from opposite direction.

For all such eventualities only a normal safe speed gives you response time and opportunity. In developed countries exclusive high speed corridors are there; which are designed for such requirements and no obstructions can be found there. Day to day accidents in our Express Highways are the indicator that our drivers are not ready for such types of facilities - many accidents have happened while drivers do test drive and check the maximum possible speed they can drive. It is high time till we establish a proper driver training infrastructure in our country and ensure that all drivers are trained before officially issuing them license. Our speed limit should be strictly fixed at 100 KM/ Hr max in such expressways and accordingly all other NH and SH should have 80 as the limit.

CHAPTER ELEVEN

UNDERSTAND BRAKING OF VEHICLES

Kill your speed; not others and yourself.

Defensive Thinking No 11 : I understand the importance of regulation of speed in such a way that a need for sudden braking never arises and I plan my speed accordingly.

Speeding and braking go together yet they are exactly opposite. Speeding creates an unsafe situation as discussed but it also makes it difficult for the driver to stop the vehicle safely when required. Braking in all modern vehicles have got a major improvement and majority of the 4 wheelers are even provided with ABS technology which prevents skidding of vehicles by not allowing the wheel to stall. This system is now available in high end bikes also. Disc Brakes have become a common feature in most of the vehicles.

While braking, one has to be very careful and the factors that affect the performances are speed, brake mechanism, tyre condition, road condition, air pressure in the tyres, weight of the vehicle, curvature, pillion rider etc. If you apply front brake only, your dynamics will be different and if you do it while turning the vehicle it may slip also. On a surface, which is slippery due to presence of dust or mud – even if you just apply brakes casually, your chances of slipping will be there, without any reason.

So the best possible driving on road is to avoid a requirement of sudden braking; then all these situations that create an accident causing scenario will automatically get avoided.

Driver should always avoid applying only front brake of a two wheeler at speeds; both front and rear or only rear should be the procedure – if the 2 wheeler has no good front brake. By applying sudden brake a driver is simply stalling the vehicle and that anyhow will destabilize the vehicle and speed & other factor mentioned above will decide the extent of change in the dynamics of your bike. A defensive driver will never change the direction of vehicle much while braking and if he find the bike is skidding, he just slightly releases the brake; provided however; he has got this much time to think and react.

A sudden braking requirement in curve will completely jeopardise all your preparation in this regard, speed control is the ultimate saviour. All these situations are to be avoided and ultimate aim of any driver should be to, start and complete a trip; without any unpleasant incidences.

Never assume the brake lights of vehicle ahead as functional and consider that as an indication for your assessing the gap between two vehicles. Your judgement should be as per actual visible physical gap between the two and your vision only should be final.

CHAPTER TWELVE

CHANGING THE LANES ABRUPTLY

These lane lines can be your lifelines too

Defensive Thinking No 12 : I promise I will never change the lane suddenly.

On roads we can see many drivers driving in zig zag fashion when they find some open stretch and this sometimes becomes their habit and can land them in difficult situations occasionally.

In a video game the joy stick gives us control on speed and direction of the vehicle; you can reduce the speed but not stop it immediately. On roads a driver has control of the speed, direction and additionally they are provided with brakes to stop; if they want. In video games we invariably manoeuvre using direction keys only and try to finish the game somehow. In a video game it's a race and our aim is to win, all other drivers are our competitors. Unfortunately, on roads also many drivers behave the same way. This approach in handling the road traffic situation is one of the major reasons for our accidents. In video games you have many lives, on roads - you have just one; which you have to protect at any cost.

Normally, fear of a possible accident makes a driver take all the correct actions on the road. On roads many drivers can be seen driving so casually without any fear, which scares other drivers and such drivers completely jeopardise the safety of the road at that moment. For many drivers the brakes don't exist in the vehicle; they simply clear the road using steering or handle; all they want is just an opening; many times they succeed; sometimes - perish.

On roads the traffic is designed to move straight along the road and any sudden change in direction is considered as an aberration – a wrong move. On roads other drivers expect us to behave in a reasonably fixed pattern. Lane changing is an important traffic requirement and it has to be done in a planned way with proper signalling; all defensive drivers does this way.

While driving, many times a situation comes; where we have to deviate from the line - to protect ourselves from hitting the vehicle ahead. This is the time where most of the drivers prefers to deflect the vehicle by changing the direction and not apply brake, to remain in same line.

A safe driver always remains in same lane and he does it by applying brakes (since he always maintains a safe gap in front of his vehicle) – a lane changing is a very special requirement and he maintains a proper protocol for that. In all developed countries, accidents are controlled by maintaining lane discipline by all drivers. There also whenever there is a violation, a potential for a possible accident develops. In our road this violation can be seen very frequently.

On roads sometimes we may find drivers; who give signals and instantaneously change direction; without giving time to others for even acknowledging the signal – with no time to react. A lane changing requires advance planning, signalling, confirming that your intention is known, ensuring that the intended lane or road is clear of vehicles or people, ensuring that you have all the peripheral views also – after ensuring all this; a lane change is initiated.

At high speed you may sometimes find yourself behind a slightly slow moving vehicle, which may prompt you for a lane change. This situation is where many accidents happen on the road – your first actions should be to slow down slightly and maintain safe distance from the vehicle ahead, then invoke a lane change procedure.

One thing you should never forget is that, in our road conditions; drivers can overtake you from either side, and many vehicles may be parked along the roads. Your assumption that the rightmost lane is the fastest lane – may be wrong and you will find a very slow moving vehicle there. Road accidents also happen due to preconceived notions of the driver about other driver's expected standard behaviour pattern on the roads; that doesn't always happen.

What is for sure is and which will definitely save a life on the road is – Drive purely based on your actual visuals of the conditions on the road. Standard visibility norm one can set should be 500 metres on highways, if a driver is able to see around 500 metres on the road straight - he is safe. If his visibility is restricted below this; due to a curve or a moving vehicle ahead or due to darkness or for any other reason – the driver should slow down and wait in same lane for improvement in visibility.

A train or an aeroplane - don't have any traffic around them but still they remain on a straight line path, train is guided in a track only; then definitely on roads where a number of vehicles and other obstructions are found-remaining in lane becomes a supreme requirement. The possibility of an accident itself comes down as soon as most drivers start moving on a straight line.

Lane changing is such an important issue that a safe driver should make it a practice to observe the side mirrors, for even a small deviation- in his path. This practice will help him in slow traffic areas and corners of the road, when he may be intending for a normal free left turn; but still a driver may appear from the left side - trying to overtake.

CHAPTER THIRTEEN

NEVER OVERTAKE IN CURVES – JUST LIKE THAT.

Defensive Thinking No 13 : I promise that I will never Overtake in a Curved over without planning.

Overtaking a vehicle as such is a special activity on a straight stretch itself; and when it is to be done on curves, it always has to be done in a planned way carefully. But for the drivers, obsessed with video game style of driving, who prefer to use steering and handles to negotiate most of the traffic situation; as soon as they see a vehicle ahead, the first thing comes to mind is to deflect the vehicle and just overtake from any side.

This attitude of drivers is contributing to many fatalities on the road. These drivers simply go and hit any incoming vehicle that comes from the opposite side, which gives them no escape route; putting themselves and the other drivers in trouble. As such overtaking on normal roads is a tricky job, visibility problems in curves make overtaking in curves very special for the driver.

If the road is turning towards your right then the visibility may be still better but if the road is turning towards left, then the visibility is a real issue. As per our own norm; 500 metres - if the road is not visible then the driver should stay put at the same speed behind the vehicle and wait for an opportunity. While overtaking in a curve; a defensive driver simply waits till he gets a straight stretch and visibility of 500 metres before initiating an overtaking action.

The vehicle driver you are planning to overtake also has to be involved in the process, his support is very crucial. He also can warn you about the vehicles coming from opposite direction. In fact if you patiently wait behind a driver; they themselves provide you a safe passage - our all long route drivers follow this practice. You too can make this a habit.

If a clear visibility is not there, then you can never be certain of a vehicle not coming from the opposite side. Also invariably you have to keep your speed low to remain at a safe distance from the vehicle you are planning to overtake. On curves your focus will be there for overtaking the vehicle and any obstruction in front of the vehicle you are planning to overtake, may force that driver to apply brakes, putting you in danger.

After overtaking it is very important that the driver is not placing himself immediately in front of the vehicle he had just overtaken. While coming to main road after after overtaking, maintaining a safe clearance between two vehicles is very important, otherwise after overtaking there will be a collision between the two vehicles.

As a standard, overtaking has to be done from the right side of the vehicle only. If you are left with no option but to overtake from Left Side Only, do it as a very special case very cautiously. Overtaking from the wrong side - from the left side is very dangerous on curves, particularly if the turning is towards the right. Our roads are not cleaned regularly on edges (shoulders) - any obstruction, heap of dust, or just a narrow roads stretch etc. creates a unsafe situation when a driver tries to overtake from LEFT.

CHAPTER FOURTEEN

HEAVY VEHICLE HAZARDS

Overtaking heavy vehicle.

Defensive Thinking No 14 : I promise that I will take adequate care before overtaking a Heavy Vehicle.
"Carefulness costs you nothing. Carelessness may cost you your life."– Safety saying

Overtaking any vehicle is a special requirement and it has to be done in a planned way. Riders of two wheelers on the road can be seen taking actions spontaneously without ever assessing the possible threat, while overtaking a Heavy Vehicle.

If a driver overtakes from the right side or even in unavoidable situations from left side of a heavy vehicle, he or she should ensure that the stretch where they are going to do this overtaking provides them sufficient clearance to do so. Many of our drivers look for minimum possible clearances and go ahead with overtaking. A small projection in vehicle as the mirror itself, a pillion rider shaking the vehicle or any obstruction on road, or a projection in the vehicle you are overtaking, suddenly your bike itself is stopping due to some reason; anything can cause an accident. In all such accidents the rider goes under the wheels of the heavy vehicle only.

Never overtake if sufficient clearance is not there in - your both sides, this is most dangerous act of ignorance that is happening on our roads. Those riders who go from left side may find themselves sandwiched between edge (shoulder) of the road and heavy vehicle – never forget both the edges of the road is the place where all dust will accumulate and you just cannot maintain your balance there. During rains, it becomes slippery too.

Always wait for right opportunity with clear visibility, then only overtake. On our roads - 4 wheeler drivers also take a lot of chances while overtaking. Overtaking can be done very safely if we just show some patience.

Better to be safe than sorry - from Heavy Vehicles

Defensive Thinking No 15 : I understand it is my responsibility to keep myself safe from a Heavy Vehicle.
On roads, there is a very thin line between life and death.
On roads we will find all types of vehicles and we quite frequently hear about heavy vehicles hitting a two wheeler from behind, or from side. In our country an unsaid rule is there, after an accident, normally the first blame goes to heavy vehicles among the two.

We must first understand the dynamics of a heavy vehicle like a truck or bus before moving further. These vehicles are bigger in size and through experience only the driver will have full idea of the length and breadth of the vehicle. We know that the seat of the driver is located in the front right side and diagonally opposite extreme end is nearly 12 to 13 metres away. Majority of area around the vehicle (except front) is visible to the driver through the mirror only. We know the objects seen in the mirrors are closer than they appear – means; there is always a possibility of misjudgement from the driver's end.

These black areas are actually blind spots for a HMV driver and it is very much possible that he may miss a car, bike or even a pedestrian while driving, if they are in this zone. Bike and pedestrian, particularly in slow speeds are more at risk.

These vehicles are already heavy and carry materials that make the total weight of the vehicle in the range of 30 Tons. Science says such heavy vehicles will stop with delay due to inherent inertia involved. So there is always a chance, if you apply brakes to your small vehicles in front of such heavy vehicles; the driver of the heavy vehicle may fail to match your braking response.

While we were writing this book, one accident happened on a highway near us. A family was going by bike, husband, wife; their two children aged 6 & 8 and his brother's son aged 8 years. They had travelled a long distance and almost reached Visakhapatnam; when a truck hit them from the side. We can avoid many accidents if we try to understand the basic requirement of safety on roads and how we interpret it. Our actions and behaviours can avoid many accidents. More people sitting in two wheeler always creates a problem for the rider to control it. This accident happened as the rider could not control the bike due to fatigue, overload of 5 people and as one of their son was sitting in front of him - thus making it difficult for him to maneuver the bike smoothly.

A motor bike is for two, not for too many.

Accidents on the road are not happening without any reason; just like that. There is always a mistake that is creating the situation, for an accident – fortunately in most of the such places - there are always alert defensive drivers; who stop it from getting converted into an accident.

A heavy vehicle on the road is a potential hazard and this point should always remain in the mind of the driver while in the vicinity of a heavy vehicle. And if you happen to be a driver of a heavy vehicle; you must always keep the safety of small drivers and pedestrians in mind. **A small driver, cyclist or a pedestrian; should never go towards the inner circle of the turning heavy vehicle – a heavy vehicle driver should always be vigilant about the small vehicles or a pedestrian in the inner circle while taking turns.**

Inner circle means the vehicle is turning right and you are also in right side of the heavy vehicle, and similarly while it is taking left turn; don't remain in the left side of the heavy vehicle. Many accidents happen in this situation, as both the vehicles run parallel for some time and any obstruction may be there in curve, or a slippery surface, or simply a judgement failure from any of the driver; an accident can happen. On our roads many accidents are happening in this situation; where a heavy driver is taking turn and a two wheeler going straight (not turning) from the inner circle - these heavy vehicles simply overrun them. **Never remain in inner circle in junctions.**

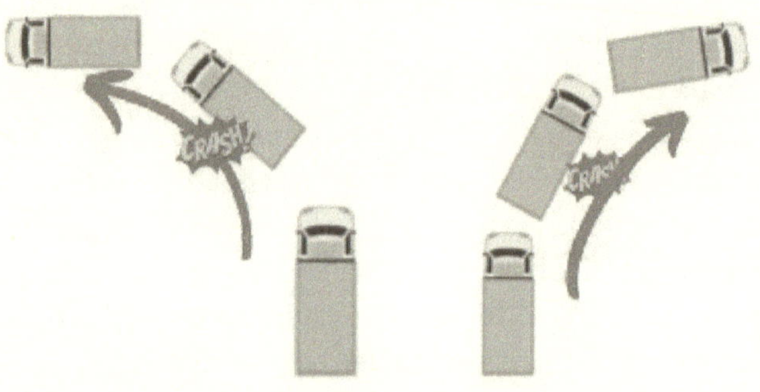

Never remain in the inner curve of a turning vehicle

Sometimes; in a junction a two wheeler driver goes in between a heavy vehicle and edge of the road - where the gap is just sufficient for his vehicle, when the heavy vehicle is in stopped condition. This heavy vehicle may turn when the traffic starts; many accidents happen when the two wheeler drivers find themselves squeezed between these heavy vehicles and road side walls or hand railings – and they can go under the wheels. Never place yourself in a tight position, where there is no escape route.

A defensive driver; will always keep a safe distance from heavy vehicles and never run two wheeler near a heavy vehicle – side by side, for a longer duration closely.

Killer wheel gaps in heavy vehicles

Defensive Thinking No 16 : I understand hazards involved with the open gap between the wheels of a Heavy Vehicle and I will keep myself away from them.

Safety is Everybody's responsibility but, First - it's my responsibility

Another important reason for not driving near a heavy vehicle is the gap between their front and rear wheels. Many types of heavy vehicles are there on the road; trucks, trailers, long vehicles, buses; among them trailers and long trucks have a very dangerously wide gap between front and rear wheel. Many accidents happen where the victim goes directly between these wheel gaps. How they reach there will be discussed separately; but as a defensive driver one must understand the danger of these gaps and stay away from them at any cost.

At the same time authorities may address this issue of guarding the gap safely, to protect many lives in similar accidents. In this book we are advocating only the prevention of accidents and therefore our aim as a defensive driver - should be to stay safely away from these gaps. We have already discussed a situation where a rider remains in the inner circle while a heavy vehicle taking a turn, these behaviours are potential danger for rider going under the wheel gaps.

Understand the danger of moving between two running vehicles

Defensive Thinking No 17 : I will never move between two running vehicles if it is not safe.

Short Cuts, Cut Shorts your Life

While driving on the roads a driver gets in a situation where he may be required to pass between two, side by side moving vehicles or vehicles overtaking each other – immediately an alarm signal should warn the driver about the moving danger on the road. This is the situation where many accidents happen on the road; and after a collision with one of the vehicles; if the person happens to be on a 2 wheeler – he may possibly go under the wheels also.

Youngsters, when they find themselves in such a situation; it thrills them and they always try to venture between the two. A safe driver should always remember that both the front drivers are not aware about this third driver's plan to go between them. They are already busy in overtaking each other and there is always a possibility that while doing so; they may reposition themselves too on the road. There will be a very narrow passage between the two moving vehicles, which will be too risky to pass through. *Imagine; exactly in that situation the bike stops due to some reason.*

The driver who attempts a passage between the two front vehicles; always assumes that both drivers will continue to drive the way they are doing now – which sometimes may not happen in the real road conditions.

A safe driver will wait for them to overtake and settle, then only proceed after ensuring his own safety.

Moving between vehicles is an unsafe act, yet this is done by many two wheeler riders. But one of the 4 wheeler driver of can observe this situation in mirror in advance. Otherwise also whenever two 4 wheelers are passing side by side; both the drivers should additionally keep a possibility of a 2-wheeler trying to go in between in their mind. We can protect them; even though they are wrong.

CHAPTER FIFTEEN

WHY ALWAYS PILLION RIDERS ?

Defensive Thinking No 18 : I understand the hazards involved in carrying a pillion rider sitting with both legs towards one side and I will take extra precautions.

Two wheelers are designed to carry two persons and the pillion rider should always sit with legs on both sides of the seat. But in our conditions ladies and senior citizens normally sit with their legs one side in the pillion. This makes them a very unbalance weight, on a two wheeler, causing many accidents.

A defensive driver should always keep this point in his mind and should never over speed or make zigzag movements on the roads with such pillion rider sitting; particularly if the person sitting behind is bulkier than the driver himself.

While a pillion rider who sits with legs on both sides of the seat is able to lock themselves with the seat properly; a one side sitting person finds it difficult to lock their position on bike. It becomes difficult for a driver to move in areas where he is required to move slowly; frequently keeping legs on ground to stop and start.

Many accidents involving a pillion rider have this reason of improperly sitting pillion rider, and a defensive driver should act accordingly. We can even see on roads, drivers carrying senior persons who sit with their legs on one side of the seat and holding some items in their hands. We have many accidents involving this pattern of sitting on a two wheeler, legs one side and not holding on to bike even with one hand.

All the information's given are reasons which can cause an accident on the road; the idea is not to advise drivers to stop carrying such pillion riders. We should identify this as an unsafe situation that needs our extra precautions; if we cannot avoid it altogether. On our roads we can sometimes find two such pillion riders sitting and riders speeding the vehicle, normally.

Most of the accidents that happen in this situations are happening, as the pillion rider simply losses their balance somehow and fall towards back side. In this type of accidents head injuries are more or the victim directly goes under the wheels of a passing four wheeler vehicle nearby. Many accidents happen when the rider takes right turn or right U turn, the pillion rider sitting with their legs one side, falls back with head hitting the road first. **This is not an ordinary situation we are talking about; we possibly fail to identify it as a cause.**

Right in front of my eyes; in 2014, a young boy was carrying his mother and aunt like this on an empty road. He was passing by the side of a truck, where unfortunately a small hump also was there on the road - all three went directly in between the wheels; none survived.

CHAPTER SIXTEEN

DRIFTING TOWARDS RIGHT IN RIGHT TURNS

Defensive Thinking No 19 : I will remain in the left side of the road, while turning right in a 2 - way road.

Rules are for compliance, Not for Violation

Every driver's first driving lesson is to keep the vehicle on the Left Side of the road and normally all of us practise this. Have you ever noticed that many drivers, on a single two-way road; when they take a RIGHT turn, without knowing, unmindfully drift towards the right side of the road?

This failure of the driver to stick to their side is one of the major cause of road accidents in our country. Because the position to which the driver is going, is the Left side for the vehicles coming from opposite side, the correct position for them. This driver will have a direct collision with the incoming vehicle.

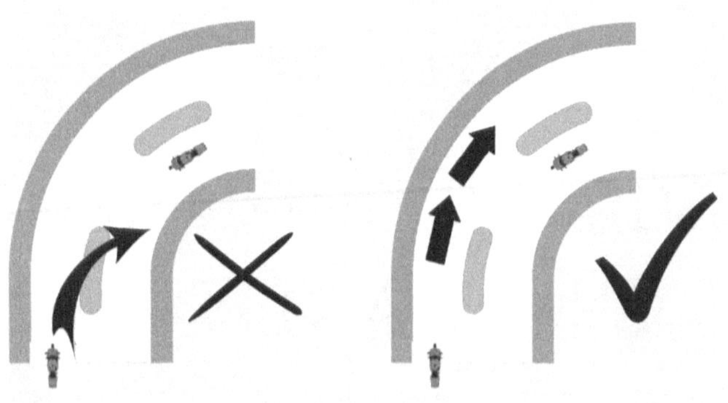

Never drift towards Right while taking a Right Turn

A safe driver always sticks to his side of the road, while taking a right turn and leaves enough space for the other vehicles to pass safely. In our first point we have mentioned about Consideration for others. If a driver just follows that religiously, automatically many other points like this, the driver need not remember.

Authorities should clearly mark the middle of all single roads along with a clear arrow marking for the path of turning curvature to be followed by the drivers; - accidents will start disappearing from our roads.

CHAPTER SEVENTEEN

NIGHT DRIVING HAZARDS

A defensive driver will always ensure adequate rest to himself and will be extra careful while carrying a group of people, particularly at night time.

Defensive Thinking No 20 : I will take sufficient rest and will take extra precautions if I have to perform a Night Driving.

Night, doubles traffic troubles

Accidents that make headlines and grab our attention are normally the accidents; where number of casualties are more. Recently 7 MBBS students died in a car accident in Maharashtra, in 2014 in Andhra, a joint family of 21 people perished in an accident, where the vehicle was driven by one of the family members only, while coming back from a pilgrimage.

Every next day you can find such accidents making headlines. These are the accidents are purely avoidable and if properly educated. We have to understand its cause - exercise caution and remain vigilant.

Such accidents happen on the roads for obvious reasons – inadequate rest to the driver, over speeding, distraction, or sometimes influence of alcohol. Again we will not go into details how it has happened. Our aim is to create defensive drivers who will be empowered with proper decision making ideas to prevent such accidents. These are the trips; which are planned to fail, an accident is inevitable. If a group assumes that everything will go normal in their trip and go ahead without any safety, then chances of accidents will be more.

Our preparations should be such, that no trip can go wrong as far as safety is concerned. A group planning for a pilgrimage or any group trips - should totally chalk out the plan; including how much time the driver is taking rest. This type of night travel plan is okay if it is in a train; but in a vehicle the driver, who has to perform the night driving, if not provided with sufficient rest – will put the entire group at risk.

Drivers will be accompanying them during the entire pilgrimage or trip, without any rest. During night while returning, all will go to sleep leaving alone, the lone driver to decide their fate. Never forget that in planes and trains, two persons - continuously monitor the journey, but on the road the same driver has to take the responsibility of all driving operations - so the group should never leave him alone. In regular bus travel, this type of issues will not arise; those long route buses may have two drivers also.

There are many instances where the driver is forced to speed up, to compensate for the delay caused by the group, to meet a deadline. A defensive driver will never mix the time constraints and safety, No delay can be compensated by taking undue risks. Many accidents are happening on the roads when the driver rushes to reach on time after a delay. Planning proper travel schedule is the most important aspect of safe driving.

For a defensive driver, whenever such a situation comes; he immediately plans for the safety of entire trip, particularly the return plan. If at any point of time he finds that he is not in a position to drive any further due to tiredness or sleepiness; he simply stops the vehicle in a secured place and breaks for a rest.

In such types of trips when a group known to each other go together; lot of discussions happens inside the vehicle, which may cause distraction to the driver. If the driver happens to be one among the group then the chances of distraction will be more. A defensive driver; should be aware of this fact and should act in a safe manner.

If in such trips the group comprises only of male members; possibility of alcohol consumption by the team also comes into picture. A safe driver not only doesn't consume alcohol himself, but prevents others from consuming. Sometimes a stopover at a roadside hotel; offers them a chance to consume alcohol; which ultimately turns tragic in some cases. Drinking and driving should never go together.

Hurrying to reach home somehow - also sometimes forces the driver to move fast, sometimes the situation may be a continuation of some function, back home - or auspicious time to catch up as discussed earlier. A small judgement mistake at high speed can have a grave consequences.

A driver is a human being and his body certainly needs rest. Whatever may be the urgency; if it compromises the safety – Driver should never take any chance. During normal times also - may be in night or even during day time, sometime a driver may feel sleepy due to tiredness or even due to monotonous boring long trip. During such situation his mind will not be focussed and chances of missing an obstruction, a vehicle or even a pedestrian will be more; many accidents happen in this state of mind on roads. A vigilant driver will immediately take safe actions and take a brief break and a refreshing nap at some secured place before moving further.

Dangers of a closed vehicle.

Defensive Thinking No 21 : I very well understand the danger of a closed vehicle.
> *Beware of confined space hazards. It can leave you breathless.*

All modern vehicles have a perfect closed environment inside the cabin to make it soundproof and for good Air Conditioning. Though they are not air tight but practically very less atmospheric air can come in.

Those cruising for a longer distance in such closed vehicles may find themselves oxygen deprived sometimes. **Particularly, if occupants are more and - AC is ON.** Naturally all-consuming same available oxygen and exhaling carbon dioxide in a confined space; makes the environment inside, rich in carbon dioxide and the brain is deprived of the oxygen.

This problem is associated with smaller vehicles like car or utility vehicles only, which can be closed from all side; even Non-AC vehicles. Sometime due to rain or in winter, all glasses are closed in a Non- AC vehicle, this situation also can cause this problem. Bigger vehicles like buses etc will not have this issues as they have more air volumes.

Night accidents particularly involving a bigger group; has got this angle also, where a driver without any known reasons, losses his orientation due to dizziness and blurred vision.

An accident in Hyderabad, involving two Engineers on highway during rainy season is very important for all of the drivers to know. It happened while the road got inundated and many including them, decided to stop by the side of the road. During night they kept the AC on and slept inside the idling car . As the water level rose, it blocked the car's silencer exhaust pipe. Due to back pressure, the exhaust fumes somehow entered the vehicle cabin inside and both were found dead later, due to carbon monoxide inhalation.

Many accidents of this kind happen when inside a garage, someone keeps the AC of vehicle ON and sleeps in an idle running car.

We must understand this danger on road and plan in a safe manner. **We are very repeatedly telling about the awareness factor; you must know about the hazards then only you are in a position to take actions. The purpose of the book is to bring all the possible facts and hazards in front of you.**

If any safe driver finds themselves in such situation, they should periodically open the window and let the fresh air in. Never keep the AC ON and remain inside a car in a confined area; or even in a closed garage, with car engine idling. Sometimes, this situation may come, where it is unavoidable and AC is required – keep the glasses sufficiently open to have a continuous flow of fresh air; **but never inside a garage or in closed room.**

Understands the danger of Highway Hypnosis

Defensive Thinking No 22 : I know how to avoid Highway Hypnosis syndrome.

Safety is not a gadget but a state of mind

Another reason for a road accident during night time is Highway Hypnosis; a little known phenomenon in 4 wheelers. This happens while driving in a straight stretch, where a driver finds himself in an effortless driving situation, with no much work to do other than keeping hands on the steering and legs on the accelerator. Long roads with almost monotonous side sceneries, with no much change; causes the brain to switch into auto mode by shutting down its system partially and allowing only hands and legs to carry out the driving. A light music or a comfortable air conditioned atmosphere with a cosy driver chair, may also induce this condition. Driver's eyes will remain open but apparently will be staring blankly.

He will be able to perform all the requirements of driving reasonably well and can travel a good distance without remembering anything about the travel route. This is not a perfect auto pilot mode; here the brain has temporarily dissociated itself from the affairs. If the road remains trouble free and straight, it may be possible that, the driver's brain may activate after some time and with little disbelief, he may continue further.

The problem comes when there is a sudden change in the road situations, a vehicle or an animal coming or a major curve comes; the brain immediately responds and wakes up – but normally in such situations the response will be certainly a delayed one and an accident is unavoidable.

A defensive driver normally during night travels, and after seeing the surroundings - understands the possibility of such conditions and ensures that he is taking a break in every 1 – 1 ½ hours of driving, keeps the windows open for some time, and some physical activity during a break will have a good effect on the body, talking to other occupant by keeping eye on road also helps a lot.

All he has to ensure is his alertness level is intact during entire night travel.

CHAPTER EIGHTEEN

WELL-KNOWN DEVILS

Never mix drink and drive

Defensive Thinking No 23 : I promise I will never mix Drinking with Driving.

"Nothing is of greater importance that the conservation of human life." – Calvin Coolidge

Drinking and driving, drinking while driving - are much discussed topics in the road safety field and a defensive driver will never mix both - and we are not discussing much about it. But the fact remains true that this menace is taking away many many precious lives on our roads and unfortunately most victims are innocent occupants of the road, who just happened to be there at that time.

Drinking under the influence of alcohol is a menace that is killing hundreds daily in India. Person under the influence of alcohol loses his reflexes and his ability to safely navigate on the roads. Many of the head injuries caused in a two wheeler are due to alcohol consumption. A normal fall converts into a head injury, which otherwise could have been prevented by the individuals, through their reflexes. An alert mind always prevents an accident and in case of accidents - takes corrective steps for personal safety.

Distractions

Defensive Thinking No 24 : While driving or riding I will fully focus on Road and will not allow any distraction.

"Arrive alive, don't text and drive."

In the present digital world, where connectivity has reached to all the corners of world; most of us try to remain connected all the time. Cell phones thus have become a major distraction for the drivers and are one of the major causes of accidents. A distracted mind engrossed in a cell phone may take away eyes from the roads for more than 3 seconds and a vehicle travelling at 60, 80 and 110 KM / Hr can travel 17 metres, 22 metres and 30 metres in 1 second respectively.

When we start talking over a cellphone while driving, one third of our attention, is lost in the conversation. While driving with only two thirds of attention, it is always possible that we may miss certain hurdles and obstructions on the road and which can become a reason for an accident. Never be under the false impression that keeping your eyes on the road while talking over phone, gives you required attention on roads.

Many incidents happen due to texting while driving. Drafting a message requires your complete attention which includes both eye and brain. While texting the driver is simply taking the eye and attention from the road, which means the driver is completely dissociating themselves from the traffic environment - an open invitation to an accident.

A small distraction can make a driver travel a long distance without noticing the hindrances on the road. A defensive driver understands the danger of taking eyes off the roads. Distraction is not only from the electronic gadgets but bending for taking some material – water etc; talking to someone by bending neck – any activity that requires a driver to take his eyes off from the road is considered as a Distraction.

For smooth driving a driver continuously has to adjust his steering, to keep vehicle aligned to the road and guide it safely. If one takes his or her eye for even a second the road situations will have a different look.

We can even see riders on two-wheelers; continuously talking on cell phone by either holding it in one hand, or by stacking it inside the helmet or just pressing it against the shoulder by bending the neck. This is a very unsafe act and if the phone is so urgent; the rider should simply stop the bike and finish the call or should take the call only after reaching the destination. No call may be important than our own safety on the road. This habit of riders is causing many accidents on the roads.

Another thing one should remember is, the direction in which we turn our head, without keeping eyes on the roads; the vehicle starts drifting in that direction; and this happens unknowingly.

Nowadays most of the roads have illuminated rumble strips to alert a driver about drifting and reaching the edge of the road, yet the eyes of the driver; constantly on the road has - no substitute and it will not allow the vehicle to drift. In a fraction of a second the road scenario sometimes changes, at that instance a distracted driver cannot respond in the expected way.

Apart from above one more important aspect of distraction is **Inattentional Blindness**. In this process while driving or riding, if your mind sways towards more important things or discussion or an important issue back home; unknowingly your mind starts completely focussing on that subject. You may miss many obvious obstructions on the road with open eyes - and it results in an accident.

Drivers very frequently lose their attention on the road, many times it happens that they drive for several kilometers unknowingly in auto mode while their mind remains busy in doing some important planning or thinking. Inattentional Blindness is your inability to spot a visible hazard on the road because your attention was focussed elsewhere. This happens while a driver handles a situation which is perceived to be more important for the driver, for example ordering some thing over voice commands, or instructing some important thing to someone over phone or simply answering some important question to someone inside the vehicle itself - these are some reason which required attention of your mind as well.

While handling such situations the driver's attention is lost and they fail to focus on the driving environment and may miss many things like a slowing vehicle ahead, a stopped vehicle on the road or any such hazards on the road. The phenomenon can trigger as an afterthought also, resulting from a cell phone discussion you just had.

When the driver is not driving with full concentration required, due to some reasons - like he is typing a message on phone, or engrossed in talking over phone, or he is thinking about something very important. Suddenly if in infront of him if a very small obstruction comes, his reaction will be overwhelming and he may cause an accident.

In normal circumstances, he will be able to see all the obstacles in advance and all his reactions will be a planned one. He will be able to overcome and handle even toughest abstractions flawlessly. While you are at the helm of the affair, driving should be your only important work on the road and you should be associated with the jobs, that are connected with driving.

If you are not directly involved with driving, still you should ensure that you are not involving the driver in any important discussion, which may result in Inattentional Blindness for the driver and indirectly affect you.

Suddenness

Defensive Thinking No 25 : I will not take any abrupt decisions on roads.

Stop accidents, before they stop you.

On roads every activity has to be done in a planned way; for suddenness, on road - there is no place. Many of the accidents happen on the road just because the doors of stationary vehicles are opened suddenly by the occupant. All safe drivers of the road; who drive by the side of a such stationary vehicle, should keep all these aspects in their mind. They should even expect that the vehicle may be started suddenly by the driver and for their safety, should maintain a safe distance.

Many drivers after parking the vehicles just open the doors, it is not only the driver; any other occupant of the vehicle also can make this mistake. Normally the vehicle is parked on the side of the road; the problem comes when the door, towards the traffic side of the road is opened;

without observing the incoming vehicles.

In Netherlands, this aspect is taught as part of curriculum in schools. The occupant has to open the door using the further hand; means if you are opening the right side doors – use left hand and for left side door – right hand. This way while opening the door, complete body of the occupant turns and they will have a clear view of the area towards which they are going to open the door. **VERY SIMPLE YET PRACTICAL APPROACH.**

The requirement of safe road etiquette from anyone is - without having a clear view of the people and vehicles around – No doors of the any vehicles should be opened - and this aspect we have to educate to our family members very clearly.

All drivers before stopping the vehicle should very clearly remind the occupants about it before opening the door and allowing them to get down .

Sometime, a need comes for a driver to move across the road, or after starting from parking position - for taking a U turn and crossing to opposite road. We can see many drivers; without properly observing the traffic around, suddenly turn the vehicle. Many accidents are happening on roads due to this mistakes, a straight coming vehicle directly comes and hits this turning vehicle. In this situation the driver has to follow all the protocol that is discussed for a Lane Changing.

Slow down at the edge before entering the main road.

Defensive Thinking No 26 : I will always slow down and if required stop before entering the main road.

Safety is not automatic, think about it.

Traffic conditions in internal roads and main roads are entirely different. Speeds of vehicles and number of vehicles are more in a main road. Whenever a driver approaches a main road from a branch road or side lanes; he should slow down and stop if required, assess the traffic in the main road – make a safe entry for him - then only should proceed and merge in the stream.

This in fact should be followed for all the road entries, be it a branch or a main one. Whenever; we approach a new road, the visibility of the area has to be ensured first – this is only possible by slowing down. In the internal roads, due to constructions and encroachments – visibility; otherwise also, remains very poor, on corners. By developing a habit of this kind, by all drivers, our safety can be ensured in many other situations also. Many drivers simply enter in the road without following any of these safety procedures, lot of accidents happen due to this behaviour.

Authorities if provide a clear line markings on all such branch roads, just before the edge of the road ahead, at entry point; over period of time slowly this message will etch in to the minds of the drivers. We have line markings in main junctions but other internal roads are left to the judgement of drivers only. But a safe driver should always draw an imaginary lines in their mind; for their own safety.

Never slow down or stop on highways abruptly

Defensive Thinking No 27 : I will never suddenly slow down or stop in the middle of a highway.

Highway or a Freeway – is the place where flow is the essence of safety. All cruise in the same direction without much deviation in their path. In this situation any sudden slowing down of a moving vehicle without adequate precaution, immediately creates an unsafe situation for others. These stoppages may not be intentional always, sometimes a breakdown; but they create a scary scenario or sometimes a cascading sequence of accidents in the freeway.

As a highway driver, one must always be prepared for such scenarios and keep sufficient gap from the vehicle ahead and behind to tackle such eventuality. Also any planned stoppage in between the road should never be done and if situations demands – try best to have a safe stoppage keeping the vehicles behind in mind and clear from road immediately.

Not exaggerating; but on our roads; drivers stop the vehicles just to talk to each other in busy traffic; it never occur to them as a potential hazard for them or to other road users. During night standing on roads like this can cause many accidents, not always all vehicles will have a functional tail lamps. Driver may miss the vehicle and can just crash on these vehicles.

Sometimes it may so happen that requirement to stop comes suddenly, like you see someone known, a bus driver see a passenger, or you miss your stop. Immediate an alert driver will take appropriate step that will avoid an accident. He will assess the situation in totality and will definitely not stop immediately, but in a planned way; slightly ahead - safely.

In freeways sometimes a driver misses to track their Exit Road and then after seeing the Exit, decides to take a turn or slows down - this action has caused many accidents on highways. This mistake will risk sometimes many lives and result in cascading chain of accidents on roads. **The driver should opt for the next Exit and come back.**

Never drive on the wrong side of the road.

Defensive Thinking No 28 : I will never drive on the wrong side of the road.

Driving on the wrong side or opposite to the direction of flow are some dangerous practices which very often happens in our roads. Just to save some distance or time or fuel; people take this step and create a very unsafe scary situation on the road for others and cause many accidents. It's very unfortunate, but even many heavy vehicle drivers do this on highways. They all assume that by **Switching ON** the headlight, Safety of all can be ensured.

A safe driver will never go in a wrong direction or a wrong side; it's the mind-set; which has to be changed. The gain is not worth the Unsafe Scenario it creates on Road .

Why do many drivers hit a stationary vehicle, or a standing vehicle in a curve?

Defensive Thinking No 29 : I will always ensure that a safe corridor is there in front of me, if not; I will simply slow down.

If you think you are the best driver, then you better be aware.

First of all, as discussed on different occasions in the books, parking of vehicles on the road is a very important safety requirement and on a freeways no one should park their vehicle. The awareness level of drivers in this regard is so poor that recently during night time a driver was found checking something under the bonnet, under the street light, at extreme right side of the road - the fastest lane of a busy road. Upon enquiring he clarified that for light he had parked the vehicle there and there was no major problem with the vehicle, he just heard some unusual sound. We stood there and got the vehicle cleared from the freeway and explained the importance of not stopping in such places.

Similarly if a vehicle gets stuck in a curve, it is the responsibility of the driver to somehow take it out, provide a safe parking space and till such time take care of other vehicles coming in the same line, by making clear distinctly visible alert signs, from a safe distance behind.

But for a regular driver till he reaches up to the location, the driving condition remains a routine one and then suddenly a stationary vehicle appears from nowhere. Here comes the role of the Defensive drivers. The driver should keep his speed, within a safe limit; which will always giving him a clear visibility of 500 metres on highways. If he sees a curve and finds that the curvature is restricting his view and it's coming down below 500 metres; he will slow down.

If he observes that he is passing from an area where both side houses are there and light is not so good - he will come to a safe speed. This, **500 metres of clear visibility** always ahead of him will be his safety shield - which will protect him from all such wrong parkings. He will ensure that this shield is always existing intact ahead of him, by fine tuning his speed.

Many times, a driver stops the vehicle due to some breakdown on highways and without providing proper danger signals on the road, simply starts attending the breakdown. There are many accidents when other drivers sometimes fail to see it in time and directly crash on the vehicle. A safe driver will provide a danger signal well ahead of the spot and alert the other drivers, giving them sufficient time to react.

Whatever may be the situation, as a safe driver you should be prepared for all such emergencies. Others may do mistakes on road; but its our responsibility to save our precious life. So never compromise on safety norms and Keep a Safe Visible gap infront always.

Accidents on Bridges

Defensive Thinking No 30 : As soon as I see a bridge or a narrow road; immediately I will slow down, and drive safely.

Many accidents happen on bridges; and over speeding in that area is the reason for such accidents. Sometimes, the bridge happens to be at the end of curve and drivers maintaining the same speed in the curve may fail to hold on to the road due to centrifugal force.

Near the water sources under the bridge; sometimes many animals may be there, they also can come in front of a driver – who in turn to save them – may turn the steering. Sometimes due to tiredness; the driver may drift too. Whenever we see a bridge, we should come down to a safe speed. On a bridge; space will be limited and if any unsafe situation is created by other vehicle, or any other person or animal on a bridge – a possibility of turning steering and hitting the railing while trying to save them, will be always there. Invariably one should slow down at the entrance and exits of the bridges; as these are places from where suddenly an animal or a person may come to road directly or possibility of a hump on that location.

No HORN PLEASE

Defensive Thinking No 31 : I will not blare the horn unnecessarily and will try to drive more with visuals what I see on the road.

HORN PLEASE is **OK** if it is done for Safety of people, saving a life, alerting the distracted people on free roads, or for compliance of rules on ghat roads, blind turns etc.

But for making our way if we are blaring HORN, it means that we are trying to force our vehicle from an area where some hazard is already there. Average speed of the vehicle is actually slow in the zone, and we should not try to overspeed. We have to actually slow down in that zone and wait till we get a clear way out.

We all have been watching the display of letters "HORN PLEASE" behind all the trucks - right from our childhood. This message has gone so deep rooted in the society that; driver stopped using their eyes on the road, whether the requirement is there or not – a Horn is always there. We blow horn, collectively, as soon as Traffic Signal goes Green – assuming the person ahead has not observed it. The farthest driver puts his best effort, to push all the drivers ahead of him and keeps on blaring horn - till they cross the junction.

For overtaking – they just blow horn and overtake; no need to monitor other safety conditions is the general attitude. Or else they will keep on blaring horns behind you; whether you are in a position to give side or not, is immaterial for them.

In modern vehicles with ACs and closed glasses, a horn may be audible but should not be taken for granted as - heard. Road traffic moves with eye visibility, and our priority should always be to practise visuals as feedback for our taking actions on roads. Stop using horns and avoid many accidents & sound pollution, as it will enhance our attention level.

91

CHAPTER NINETEEN

FREE FLOW OF THE TRAFFIC IS THE KEY

"Safety isn't expensive, it's priceless." – Author unknown

On the roads sometimes, we come across moving ambulances, a defensive driver immediately gives way to the vehicle and if required go, out of the way - to ensure smooth passage for the Ambulance.

It is the responsibility of one and all, to ensure - free flow of traffic around their vehicle. Everyone may be in a hurry to reach the destination – and any obstruction created by someone will completely throttle the flow of traffic; which will affect one and all.

Whenever there is an obstruction on the road due to any reason, immediately all drivers on our roads create new lanes - enter any space they get on the road and completely throttle the vehicular movement. Authorities struggle more, to clear the jam created by this new development, than to sort out the original issue.

Always waiting patiently in position, clears the traffic faster and people can reach their destination earlier. Easier said than done – but the situation in the country is this and patience is the only solution.

Defensive Thinking No 32 - I will Never block a Free Left. : Normally on a Junction; Left turn is free unless it is mentioned otherwise. A defensive driver never blocks the free left turn and thus contributes to the free and faster flow of traffic.

Defensive Thinking No 33 - I will always keep towards left in a junction if I have to go straight : While moving in a straight direction when the driver approaches a junction, the driver should keep himself in the left lane, and keeps the space free for drivers who take a right turn; for keeping the flow of the traffic smooth.

Defensive Thinking No 34 - I will never overtake just before Junction, if I have to turn left after that : Sometimes, a driver may be planning for a left turn in the junction and he may find himself behind a vehicle. Never overtake the vehicle and immediately take the left turn. While taking turn a vehicle may be required to slightly slow down; and by slowing down immediately after overtaking, that vehicle may be forced to brake because of you slowing down. This type of situations are causing lot of accidents on the roads; just near the junction. If you are safely away from junction then overtaking is acceptable but near the junctions; always allow the vehicle ahead to cross and as a safe driver, take left turn from behind only.

Defensive Thinking No 35 - I will always use dipper in traffic: To enable smooth flow of traffic a defensive driver puts his best efforts - he will use dipper to enable better view to the opposite driver.

Defensive Thinking No 36 - I will always park the vehicle safely, not obstructing others : He will park the vehicle in such a way that, it will not be an obstruction for any one, he will never park it on a curve. Parking a vehicle at the junction is one of the most traffic throttling mistakes done by the driver. It slows down vehicles on both sides – a driver trying for a U turn will find it difficult to negotiate.

As such parking vehicles along the roadside has to be done very safely for smooth vehicular movement - and it creates a situation where a pedestrian is forced to come on to the road, which exposes them to heavy traffic directly. It also restricts free movement of vehicles in an already narrow road and traffic movement becomes throttled and creates a situation for possible accident.

Defensive Thinking No 37 - Before starting a vehicle from a stationary position I will ensure all safety: Starting the vehicle from stationary position is a responsible action and while starting, a safe driver always ensures no vehicles are coming from behind and sufficient clearance is there in front and back side - to take out the vehicle from parking position.

Defensive Thinking No 38 - It is always safe to go from behind the animals and allow them to go freely: On roads sometimes we may find animals, some may be scared because of traffic and no driver should expect the animals to behave in an organised way – they should be allowed to move away smoothly without disturbance. It is always safe to go from behind the animals in such situations.

In fact a safe driver, if he finds even a pedestrian on road, he will go from their behind only. Normally with the pedestrian there may be a chance that, he can be distracted, but for a driver any obstruction in front is clearly visible to his eyes and he will be in a better position to take appropriate actions.

Defensive Thinking No 39 - I will never carry any loose items in the vehicle: A loose item on a vehicle, particularly on two wheeler or an open transport vehicle; are reasons for many accidents or near misses on the roads. Secure them properly.

Defensive Thinking No 40 - I understand the danger of long items being carried in vehicles: While transporting long items, our drivers just tie any available cloth piece and venture on roads. Long products like rods or pipes carrying vehicles, are reasons for many dangerous accidents that happen in our country. They are dangerous when they move straight; they are deadly when they take turns.

A safe distance from vehicle carrying long product is very much essential from behind. There are accidents involving such vehicles, when they apply sudden brakes due to some reason, the projected products directly pierce the vehicle that follows them and can even hit the occupants too – if the trailing driver fails to react in time. Sometimes they simply roll down and hit the vehicle coming behind.

A safe driver understands this hazard and stays away from them. Such vehicles, which have projections beyond the length and breadth of the vehicle should not be allowed to move freely on roads. A normal driver takes precautions to the extent of the dimensions of the vehicle around and but a defensive driver goes beyond.

Defensive Thinking No 41- I will wait patiently for my turn: On roads you can find drivers just willing to enter any small space available without at all bothering for the safety of others. As soon as they see the gap, even if it's about to be occupied by the eligible driver coming in straight line, they just occupy it from side and force the driver to brake and slow down. On road we have to always leave room for the designated driver in line and entry from side is the reason for many accidents and it should be avoided at any cost.

Defensive Thinking No 42 - I will take care of the pedestrian for their safety: All road junctions may not have provisions for pedestrian crossing light timings or signals; but we have to allow them to move safely. A defensive driver moves slowly in a junction not for his own safety but for the safety of others also; particularly the pedestrians. It may so happen that the signal for you may be green; but due to some unavoidable reasons some pedestrians may remain stuck in between – their safety becomes our prime responsibility too.

While crossing the road keep a keen eye on the pedestrian movements to ensure their safety. In our death count of 400 deaths per day, their numbers are considerable – which all of us know is avoidable. Fault may be from their side; still a driver can protect them. We can find pedestrians on roads with distracted attention; talking on cell phones, running to catch the bus; all these - a safe drive can cover up.

Defensive Thinking No 43 - I will always slow down in Curves: For smooth flow of traffic a safe driver will always slow down in a curve irrespective of its location; in a curve, there is always a possibility of judgement failure. In a T road, if you are entering the straight road stretch from side, then you should ensure that you are waiting on the edge of the road. After having, clear view of the straight road only, you should enter the stream. **Again remember the right of way is for the Drivers Coming straight.**

Defensive Thinking No 44 - I will always be careful of roadside parked vehicles: There may be many stretches on the roads; where on the side, vehicles will be parked and standing in line. While crossing such locations expect a vehicle suddenly starting, a pedestrian coming out or even an animal – maintain a safe distance from the edge of the road.

Defensive Thinking No 45 - I will always slow down while passing through Villages or Thickly populated areas: While passing through villages or areas, where both side houses are there, a safe driver will have a different safety norm. In these areas there is always a possibility of a stray animal coming, kids crossing the path, a cyclist coming suddenly, or a drunk man trying to locate his house – more chances of surprises are there in such types of roads.

Moving slowly and safely is the best safety precaution one can take in these areas. Basically we are moving in between their houses and it's our responsibility to ensure their safety around their house. During night time crossing through these areas may demand you to be more vigilant. Such stretches may be very less on the roads, but more accidents happen in such places.

Safe defensive driving is basically control of the vehicle speed according to road conditions and our intention is to bring all sorts of situations in front of you, so that you can easily correlate.

Defensive Thinking No 46 - I will always honor the right of way to the right person: Vehicles coming from lanes, bye lanes, joining major roads should invariably give preference to those plying in the major roads.

CHAPTER TWENTY

OTHER FACTORS

Railway crossing accidents.

Defensive Thinking No 47: In a Railway Crossing I will always take all the precautions and will never take any risk.

"The automobile has brought death, injury and the most inestimable sorrow and deprivation to millions of people." –
Ralph Nader

While driving whenever a driver sees a railway track with or without a gate; no second thought should come to his mind - the driver should invoke the safety precaution of slowing down in a planned way. A driver can see an incoming railway gate well in advance so planning should never be an issue. If the gate is closed the driver simply has to wait and allow the train to pass and the gate to open.

In our country many two wheeler riders, four wheeler drivers and pedestrians have met with gruesome accidents while attempting to cross the track by taking risks. Accidents involving school buses where many innocent lives were lost, are still fresh in our memories.

If the gate is not closed or there is no gate at all; the driver has to make his own procedure of crossing by slowing down and crossing after ensuring that the train is not there within a safe long distance, till the distance the track is visible towards the both ends.

All the roads approaching at railway crossings normally have 90 degrees of intersections; so visibility is not an issue. Accidents happen in crossings when the driver, after seeing an open gate or no gate; continues to drive at the same speed. **One should never assume a clear track as no chance of a train coming – but should always trust their own eyes.** Accidents that happen on the track are more severe in nature and casualties are very high. The accident may even derail a train and may lead to a catastrophe.

Many accidents also happen while attempting to cross the track in hurry; drivers fail to maintain their cool and in panic remain stuck over the track. Track accidents are just avoidable - should not happen at all and a safe driver never takes a chance there; in the overall safety.

A blocked visibility

Defensive Thinking No 48: I understand the danger of visibility blockages due to windscreen columns and I take adequate care to ensure that I am able to see my surroundings properly.

"An *ounce of prevention is worth a pound of cure*" –
Benjamin Franklin

A windscreen column of a 4 wheeler creates a blind spot in the driver's view of the road. Right one creates a wider blind area than the left; as it is near to your eye. Many unbelievable accidents right in front of the eyes of the drivers have happened due to this reason; particularly in junctions.

While taking a turn or U turns in a junction, drivers tend to focus more on the mirrors for their clearances. Since objects in mirrors are nearer than they actually appear; sometimes a driver may miss a two wheeler or an individual. Simultaneously, they may sometimes will not be seen by the driver due to the view blockage by the blind spot of this column and an accident may happen. As occupant of roads, all must understand the hazards involved with heavy vehicles and don't go near a turning vehicle in junctions. All defensive driver of both LMV and HMV, while negotiating such a situation - always sees from both sides of the column, slows down further for safety and bend his neck for better visibility, particularly the inner curves.

Make yourself visible

Defensive Thinking No 49: I will ensure that my vehicle is visible under all climatic conditions, I also ensure that I am able to see all the pedestrians and animals on the road.

"The real enemy of safety is not non-compliance but non-thinking." – Dr. Rob Long

Role of visibility is very important on roads, while you are in a vehicle or you are occupying the road as a cyclist or just a pedestrian. This simple issue can cause an accident despite having enough time to react, when someone fails just to see each other and react in time.

From 2016 onwards in our country Automatic Headlight ON is mandated in two wheelers as soon as the engine is made ON. This has reduced crashes involving two wheelers in many part of country particularly during the time when visibility may be low due to climatic conditions like fog or rains.

For ensuring visibility of 4 wheeler and older 2 wheelers, in such situations, a safe driver switches the lights ON.

Maintenance of all indication lamps tail lamp, reverse lamp, turning indicator lamps are very important in this direction. A driver assuming that his turning indicator is ON, takes a turn; but in reality it may not be functional, can create a situation on road.

Visibility of pedestrian is also an issue that we need to keep in mind while driving on the roads, you can observe people wearing perfect black clothes during night and venturing on roads in a very casual manner.

Pedestrians wearing light coloured clothes are better visible in night than dark dress. Cyclist should make themselves visible by wearing light cloths and now cycles are also fitted with lights.

One to the major cause of accidents on our road is the buffaloes and cows occupying the roads , during night. Buffaloes being black in colour, can not be spotted in night easily and many accidents are happening on roads due to these animals in our country.

These animals need to be organised and should not be allowed to be on roads. They move around on the roads in search of food and at fixed time , will be brought back for milking them.

These innocent animals are killing many innocent drivers; sometimes even getting killed. If a proper guideline is brought out in this direction; many lives can be saved. But as a driver while driving in night, one has to be vigilant for animals also.

Car or Boat

Defensive Thinking No 50: I will never take a chance in an overflowing bridge during rains.

"Everything you need to get that relaxed driving that brings consistency, only comes with practice."- Unknown

Sometime, during rains we may find ourselves in a situation where the bridge may be overflowing and we may be in a dilemma about whether to cross or not. We should understand that the vehicles particularly car is a completely closed cabin and it can always float in water.

While crossing such areas normally the water level initially may be less, but as you go ahead, there is always a possibility that the water may be more than your estimation. If the water level crosses above your chassis level area and if the flow is sufficient; there is always a possibility that the car may float and simply flow away along the stream.

So for the safety of person, while encountering such situation - caution is very important.

Dead Animals on roads

Defensive Thinking No 51: I will take all precautions to remain vigilant about the animal movements on the roads.

"If safety is a joke, then death is the punchline." –
Unknown

On roads many times we see dead animals, mostly dogs within city limits or wild animals, outside. **One thing we should never forget that - as a human being, we will never**

kill an animal with our vehicles; a human being - no chance. Whenever such a situation comes; our reflex will simply guide us to protect the animal and we invariably do it by applying sudden brakes or turning the steering wheel or handle.

All those dead animals are the cases, where drivers could not see the animals and they got overrun. Had the drive seen them, an accident was the only outcome. If this situation comes with a two wheeler; the severity will be more. Otherwise also by suddenly applying brakes or turning the vehicle; the person behind is also exposed to the risk with a possibility of collision.

A safe driver keeps this aspect of driving in mind and he will not drive much on the edges of the roads; particularly in night time, when visibility also is poor. These dogs; which might have been, chased away by another dog; will come on to the road so fast that, a driver may hardly get some time to react.

Ghat road

Defensive Thinking No 52: In a Ghat road I will take all the precautions and follow all protocol

Mountains are pleasure if you drive with leisure

Ghat road driving requires a special skill and knowledge. We have discussed the basics of overtaking in curves; the same is applicable. Here **always preference is to be given to the vehicle climbing up.** A climbing vehicle sometimes after stopping may not be able to pick up the momentum, due to steep climb, load, vehicle condition or may be due to driver's skill.

On ghat roads since visibility will be very restricted due to continuous turns; a safe driver here patiently waits for the most suitable opportunity before overtaking. In ghats normally the driver ahead also helps in giving a good slot for overtaking and thus they form a team.

While coming down, for heavy vehicles; to have a controlled speed - always the vehicle should be kept at lower gears, otherwise the vehicle may over speed; lower the gear slower the vehicle – higher the braking torque. For light vehicles and two wheelers also the same rule is applicable; if a driver feels that the vehicle is not coming down at a controlled speed.

Many places clearly Blow Horn boards will be there – a safe driver strictly follows those boards. During winter sometimes fog may restrict your visibility; speed has to be immediately corrected accordingly. In general on ghat roads speed will be lower than a normal road.

CHAPTER TWENTY-ONE

FREAK ACCIDENTS

"Do not think because an accident hasn't happened to you that it can't happen."– Safety saying

Sometimes some freak accident happens with no obvious reasons – some to the reason that could be identified are listed for information.

1. Drivers should ensure that all the occupants are safely sitting inside the vehicle and all the doors are secured properly. Many accidents have happened due to open doors or the occupant is still getting in – driver should ensure this physically and inform before starting.

2. While moving in two 2 – wheelers side by side , the mirrors entangles - resulting in an accident. We know case in our area when one of the driver succumbed. Otherwise also; while riding side by side - there is always a possibilility of crashing on each other.

3. A rider fails to see a speed breaker jumps on it, while the wheels are still in air he applies brakes. Upon touching ground a completely stalled front and back wheel stops him all of a sudden and a major accident happens. While

braking, this aspect should be kept in mind.

4. Many riders have habit of loosely keeping hands on the handle or they drive with single hand mostly. Such drivers when they jump a breaker unknowingly or sometimes suddenly, lose their balance and fall. If it happens to be inside a busy traffic; it can be dangerous.

5. Riders while stopping their 2 wheelers should be careful while placing their feet on the ground. In an incident, while stopping at a junction when a rider tried to keep his legs on the ground, his left leg pant got entangled to the footrest and the vehicle toppled. His head directly went inside the wheels of the truck, which was almost stopping. Loose pants are to be avoided in bikes.

6. Gearless two wheeler; has one inherent problem, after it is started; its speed is controlled only with the accelerator - No clutch . Sometimes, we make our children stand within our legs and they hold the handle for support. There are many cases when they inadvertently accelerate the vehicle, when it is in stop condition with engine idling. Whenever a rider misses the balance due to some reasons in these gearless vehicles, they unintentionally only accelerate the vehicle. One has to be careful while using such vehicles.

7. Instances of school bus or van overrunning the children after dropping then in destination is a clear negligence from drivers end; distraction and not paying attention for the complete clearance of the children is the cause.

8. Oil or grease on the road sometimes may surprise you. On roads you may find such slippery surfaces created by some spillages, if you can spot them timely and are able take corrective steps, it is okay. But if you miss and brake after reaching on top of it; you are going to slip only. Night time identifying them also will be difficult.

If you find crossing them is inevitable; just reduce the speed by accelerator only; don't apply brakes over them. Allow the vehicle to move without power, and keep the steering or handle almost straight only.

9. Loose item near your legs like bottles or sometime removing footwear to relax have caused many accidents in four wheelers, when they go under your brake pedal. We have to be careful about them.

10. Many freak accidents happen, when loose clothes worn by pillion riders get entangled in the chain or wheel sprocket. This will simply pull down the pillion rider in a running bike and many accidents happen in this situation. Recently in one video we have seen, a pillion rider to protect her from rain opens the umbrella and falls due to wind pressure.

RESCUE OPERATION ON ROADS

The rescue operation after an accident on the road is also a major road safety issue in itself. Many times it has been seen that rescuers and people busy taking the victims to the hospital, themselves get involved in accidents when suddenly a speeding vehicle comes and crashes on them. It is not always necessary that fully trained people should only come to rescue the victims of an accident. Usually people who are nearby immediately after the accident or the passengers of the vehicle that passes by - are the first to arrive at the accident site.

Specially trained security personnel have their own professional approach of handling the victims, but in India there is not much difference between a common citizen and an ambulance worker; due to lack of such special provision. The accident of the rescue team while evacuating the victims of road accidents, is also very often heard. In developed countries where security personnel are given special training to perform this type of rescue operation safely, in their vehicles they have everything to carry out such operations smoothly.

Before commencing a rescue operation the team or the member/ members involved in rescuing a victim/ victims should first ensure their own safety. As on the roads, still the movement of other vehicles may be going on and those drivers are not aware about this accident. If we fail to alert them, we will endanger other oncoming vehicles by not alerting them about these unexpected disruptions, endangering our own lives, as well as of the accident victims; who probably remain in a wounded condition till that time.

While rescuing, our first and foremost task is to secure the victims and evacuate the involved vehicle(s) from the accident site. If the road is completely closed due to the accident, then accumulation of vehicles will automatically stop the flow. But if there is space left for other vehicles to flow on the road, then it becomes necessary to warn the oncoming vehicles about the accident in advance. For this, a traffic cone is usually used, which is normally available with the rescue team only. All other vehicles are usually provided with a triangular Danger Alerting Sign with the kit. Normally one such alerting sign is provided in one vehicle; which may not be sufficient.

Alerting and warning the oncoming vehicles is done minimum about 50 meters in advance, otherwise it is possible that one of the oncoming vehicles may fail to observe this accident vehicle parked on the road and may hit them directly. Many times the driver of an oncoming vehicle may be distracted exactly at that moment of time and such drivers are dangerous.

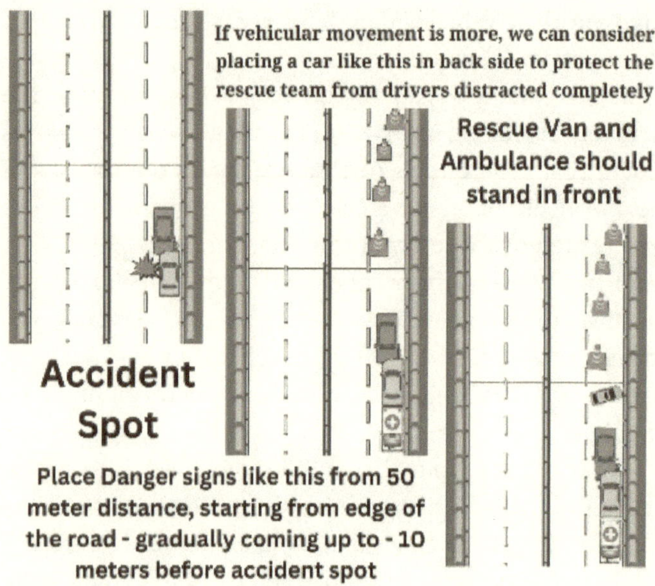

To alert other road users about the accident, normally we put up some danger signs like traffic cones or triangles, to warn from about 50 meters in advance on the road. If you do not have anything in your hand, we can use some branches from the surrounding trees, put them on the road in a triangular manner, whose picture is attached, in the diagram we have used only real traffic cones. This will help the coming vehicle to expect a blockage of the road after seeing the first warning sign and since it is gradually coming on to the road; it will not be dangerous for the oncoming vehicles. At the same time if in spite of providing a danger sign, still the driver continue to come in the same lane, he gets alerted after hitting the next cone. Specially trained team even places a vehicle across the road just 10 meters before the accident spot, so that in the worst case of the driver remaining completely distracted; still they are safe.

In a road accident where every minute is precious to save a life, many times there is no opportunity to make such safety efforts, in such situations, on humanitarian grounds our focus will always be there on for saving the victims. Nevertheless, every effort must be made to put some danger signs about 50 meters ahead to warn the oncoming vehicles and keep your own safety in mind. The idea of thinking about your own safety will normally provide you with safe situational solutions.

There are danger signs available for such road situations in the market, always keep 4 of those signs & a first aid box in your vehicle handy. Sometimes by providing first aid to a road accident victim his or her life can be saved. Take care of your own safety before handling a crash victim - one persons should be made responsible and always be a good samaritan to volunteer for such a situation.

CHAPTER TWENTY-THREE

USAGE OF PERSONAL PROTECTIVE GEAR

Helmets, seat belts, and shoes are some of the personal protective equipment (PPE) which will reduce the impact of accidents to the occupants or the riders or drivers. These are to be strictly used and in most cases they have protected the drivers in case of accidents.

However under no circumstances one should be under the false impression that these PPEs prevent an accident; these are purely engineering interventions to reduce the injury to the driver and have least impact in control of accidents.

During a two wheeler crash mostly the injuries happen to the lower part of the body but head injuries are the major reasons for fatalities involving two wheelers. A properly secured helmet saves an individual from head injuries. It is very important that the buckle of the helmet is locked properly and your helmet is not loosely fitted to your head. Otherwise the helmet will be the first object to be thrown away from your body in the event of an accident – leaving you unprotected and exposed. And no one should compromise over the quality of the helmet, as it's designed to save the most precious life of yours - a cheap helmet is equivalent to NO HELMET.

Many theories are there about individual's freedom for wearing a helmet. We have many friends living with us today, who have survived a crash as they had the helmet on their head **on that day.** In many cases the crash was caused by others mistake, a helmet will protect the individual in such cases. Glass of the helmet otherwise also protects you from many foreign flying objects. On our roads, one can spot many two wheelers, where helmet will be hung on the handle bars, only to be worn when some authorities are spotted on roads.

We know a case where a couple were travelling on a two-wheeler; the helmet was with the lady sitting behind. When they spotted police in a road Junction area; immediately rider asked wife to place helmet on his head. Which she did but unfortunately in reverse way; completely blocking the visibility for the rider. In that accident she could not survive and rider had fractured limbs.

Seat belts secures a driver in vehicles and keeps them in position in the event of a crash. High speed crashes makes a driver to fly inside a vehicle like a free object and most injuries happen when they hit the glass or other areas inside the cabin. They may even injure others, who may be sitting wearing the seat belt. Always wear a seat belt while driving. Driver can be simply thrown out of the vehicle if they are not wearing a safety seat belt.

Airbags in four wheelers are designed to save the occupants in the event of a collision. However for the airbags to save effectively it is mandatory that the occupants are wearing the seat belt also. Seat belts are considered the primary level of safety and Airbag the Secondary. It is very important that the occupants sitting in the back seat also must wear seat belts, otherwise they will not only bear the brunt of the accident but severely injure the driver also in the event of a collision.

Mirrors are very critical for monitoring the surroundings and they have to be very strictly maintained. In old vehicles only a single mirror used to be there, now both the side mirror is a must, on both 2 and 4 wheelers.

CHAPTER TWENTY-FOUR

TIPS FOR DRIVERS

- Always be thankful when people let you go at junctions, or in some way make your trip better and safe on roads, this way you'll contribute to a far more harmonious approach on roads.
- To have effective braking in your vehicle never apply clutch simultaneously while braking. Not pressing clutch will give you the required damping effect faster and better; engage clutch just to prevent the engine from stalling or stopping.
- Never carry partially filled fluids in a tanker; moving liquid inside a tanker can disturb your balance and your vehicle may topple in turns. If it's unavoidable, then you must go at a very safe low speed.

Maintenance of the vehicle.

Many accidents happen due to improper maintenance of the vehicles and not properly monitoring various parameters. We are not touching this aspect in detail, Some of the important issues that have bearing on road safety are mentioned for the benefit of the readers. Timely Routine maintenance of the vehicle ensures that the safety intervention like brakes are in order and other machinery is in good working condition and road healthiness is ensured.

Some other parameters that we have to monitor are the tyre pressure and quality of the tyre treads. Accidents are happening on the roads due to bursting of tyres in the summer season and during continuous long running - because of over pressure in them. A good tyre ensures, good grip on the road and due to ageing the rubber becomes brittle and it may giveaway in tough driving conditions.

Structural checking of the vehicle is also very important, as after certain time main chassis strength also may come down. Many cases can be seen on the roads when, cabin gets separated form vehicle, complete undercarriage or body breaking away while vehicles are on move. Road worthiness is very important and it should not be compromised – these accidents can be fatal also in many cases.

Overloading the vehicle

All vehicles are designed to carry certain specific weight in view of the safety standards. Any overloading beyond that will hamper its structural strength, it manoeuvrability, its stopping time and ability of the drivers to control it.

Small overloading of allowing 3 person in a 2 wheeler, to overloading of material in four wheeler and heavy vehicle come under the purview of such overloading and may lead to an accident due to above mentioned reasons.

CHAPTER TWENTY-FIVE

FIRST AID

First aid to victims of Road Accident

Though preventing an accident remained the prime focus of this book writing; still ultimately the aim is to save a life somehow. Life of an accident victim can be saved by timely administering the First Aid. **The 'GOLDEN HOUR', the first one hour; after the accident, is called the 'golden hour'**. If the victim is brought to the medical facility within an hour; it would be possible for the doctors to revive them and save a life.

But on road conditions it will not be possible always to take a victim to nearby hospitals within this Golden Hour. Sometime the accident may happen in such a remote location; where others will know about accidents after many hours. But it is always possible to provide a First Aid at the spot itself. Immediately first aid is if given to road accident victims during this hour, it increases the chances of their survival and even reduces the severity of injuries.

In such situation a passer-by, onlooker and other people around, can provide the first aid to the victims. However, fear of improper handling to victims which may worsens the situation, prevents many to come forward.

One of the misconceptions about road accidents death is that it happens due to sever injury and loss of blood. But reality is exactly opposite – the most common cause of death in a road accident is due to loss of oxygen supply and it always happens due to blockage of airway. Basic First Aid can be provided by anyone since it has to be done instantaneously. It takes less than four minutes for a blocked airway to cause death - so the person standing closest to the victim only can do the job on behalf of GOD. Though providing proper first aid to an accident victim is not so complicated procedure but one should be careful of the precautions in the absence of proper training.

As author is not well conversant with medical intervention procedures, all First Aid procedure that is recommended by Ministry of Road Transport & Highways, Government of India, is just reproduced for overall safety on road.

Many procedures, an individual may find it difficult to do and may hesitate to do it - on others. Here we would like to bring a very important fact that, on many occasions a family member has saved a life by doing this first aid on spot. Also; every time when our family members are on road, we may not be around. All on road, to be treated as our own family member – so that, someone in right time will think, in the same way; when our dears may be in trouble.

Following are the four medical conditions that a First Aid provider has to focus.

- Asphyxia (loss of oxygen)
- Cardiac Arrest
- Severe Haemorrhage (Bleeding)
- Other Injuries/Illnesses

First thing first

To make most use of first 4 critical minutes, we must remember to

- Make the area clear
- Take care of the victim
- Help them in reviving
- Call help

ABC rule

- Airway - Clear the airway i.e. breathing track
- Breathing - Help restore it by mouth to mouth resuscitation (we can learn through videos available in internet)
- Circulation - Stop any bleeding

Clearing Airway

- Put the victims on ground very gently and cautiously without any further aggravation to the injury.
- Turn the victim to one side.
- Loosen clothing at neck, chest and waist.
- Tilt the head back, point the face slightly down so the tongue can fall forward allowing blood and vomit to drain out.

Restoring breath - mouth to mouth resuscitation.

If the victim is still not breathing, give him artificial breathing. (We can learn through videos available in internet)

- Turn the victim onto the back and start mouth-to-mouth resuscitation immediately.
- Tilt head back, support jaw, keep your fingers clear of throat;
- With good mouth to mouth seal and your cheek sealing the victim's nose, blow into the mouth until the chest rises;
- Lift your mouth, turn your head to see chest fall and listen and feel for air escaping from nose and mouth.
- If chest does not rise, check; for blocked airway.
- Mouth to mouth seal
- Continue mouth-to-mouth resuscitation until breathing is restored. Blow every four seconds with adults and every three seconds with children.

Circulation - stop any bleeding

- Uncover bleeding wound. Stop bleeding by direct pressure on the wound with thick pad of bandage or cloth.
- Bleeding limbs should be elevated to prevent bleeding.
- Do not remove foreign objects from bleeding wound.
- Apply pads and bandage them around the wound. Do the same if broken bones are visible.

These procedures are very simple and one must keep themselves aware by observing in videos available in internets and there are thousands of cases, where a stranger has saved a life; you can be a saviour too.

About Author

A D Joshi, Author has been promoting and spreading awareness about road safety for the past more than 15 years. Death of very closely associated friends and some of their children , pains and agonies of these families - all these things have forced the author to go for bringing out this creation; so that such cruelties of fate are not happening in other families.

Most of the deaths that happen are avoidable and are happening just due to ignorance and over confidence. In fact we never think that an accident can happen to us too; if just road users start thinking of ROAD SAFETY, many accidents will just disappear from roads – and this is applicable to all the road users including a pedestrian.

A need for spreading awareness in our country is overdue and with the upcoming infrastructure improvements, we need to be more careful.

What is more painful is that unfortunately India has become the number one country in the most number of accidental deaths and this should not be acceptable to any of us. We have to certainly do our bit to take away this black spot from our forehead.

This book is the author's contribution for above and if its contents can influence someone in the country in their day to day dealings in safe road usages; it will be a great achievement for us.